Joined at the Hip

Joined at the Hip

A History of Jazz in the Twin Cities

Jay Goetting

Minnesota Historical Society Press

www.mhspress.org
The Minnesota Historical Society Press is a member of the
Association of American University Presses.
10 9 8 7 6 5 4 3 2 1
∞ The paper used in this publication meets the minimum requirements of the
American National Standard for Information Sciences—Permanence for
Printed Library Materials, ANSI Z39.48–1984.

ISBN: 978-1-68134-105-7 (pbk)
ISBN: 978-0-87351-817-8 (cloth)
ISBN: 978-0-87351-832-1 (e-book)

Library of Congress Cataloging-in-Publication Data

Goetting, Jay.
Joined at the hip: a history of jazz in the Twin Cities / Jay Goetting.
p. cm.
Includes bibliographical references and index.
ISBN 978-0-87351-817-8 (cloth: alk. paper) — ISBN 978-0-87351-832-1 (e-book: alk. paper)
1. Jazz—Minnesota—Minneapolis—History and criticism. 2. Jazz—Minnesota—Saint Paul—History and criticism. 3. Jazz—Social aspects—Minnesota. I. Title.
ML3508.7.M55G74 2011
781.6509776'579—dc22

To Dave Sletten (1955–2000)
who began chronicling the jazz history
of the Twin Cities with Kent Hazen nearly twenty years ago.

"There are only three things America will be known for 2,000 years from now when they study this civilization: the Constitution, jazz music, and baseball."

—Gerald Early *critic and essayist*

WMIN

Foreword

Leigh Kamman

Joined at the Hip: A History of Jazz in the Twin Cities heralds an intriguing record of the American jazz experience. It connects Minneapolis and St. Paul to New Orleans, Kansas City, St. Louis, Chicago, Detroit, Cleveland, New York, and at least a half dozen other American cities.

Author Jay Goetting invites you to explore through the years the regional significance of such artists as Lester Young, Oscar Pettiford, Ella Fitzgerald, Maria Schneider, Anthony Cox, Frank Morgan, Eric Kamau Gravatt, Paul "Doc" Evans, and Butch Thompson, as well as producers like Tom "Tippy" Morgan, who went on to Capitol Records and recorded artists such as George Shearing and Nancy Wilson.

As your guide, Goetting borrows on his experience as a practicing musician (double bassist) and as a writer, editor, radio broadcaster, and programmer. He knows the ropes, having toured nationally with Buddy Rich and worked with such luminaries as Doc Severinsen and Brazilian pianist Manfredo Fest. Goetting's approach is based on having lived and worked in the Twin Cities music scene and on his knowledge of the players and their history. Enriching this understanding, Jay continues to perform in both the San Francisco Bay Area and Phoenix.

What fascinates me most is the range of experience Jay Goetting brings to this project. Goetting shares the performer's view as well as the producer and administrator's vision.

You and I begin this trip when jazz emanates from a crank phonograph or airs from a crackling radio. Or live from a Mississippi riverboat docking in St. Paul, moonlit messages trumpeted by a young Bix Beiderbecke or

Louis Armstrong more than a thousand miles from the Crescent City of New Orleans.

Goetting's jazz compass points the way for us. Come along down the decades as he takes us to the ballrooms, theaters, concert halls, radio broadcasts, after-hours bistros, roadhouses, key clubs, strip clubs, and jam sessions. Live jazz presented by big and small combos challenges the local lock on popular, folk, and classical European musical culture.

I remember the depression years, when WDGY, 1130 on the AM dial, presented "White heat, y'all!" George Carson Putnam, a St. Paul Central High School student, offered pre-hip-hop exposure to the legendary trumpet player Henry "Red" Allen and Jimmy Lunceford's powerhouse big band. Said Putnam, "That's something scintillating, smooth . . . jazz, jittery jameroo."

Or it may have been Lester Young, soloing nightly and soulfully with Boyd Atkins and members of the Pettiford family at another Cotton Club, this one in the Minneapolis suburb of St. Louis Park. Or Benny Goodman's touring Camel Caravan, broadcasting live on KSTP Radio and coast-to-coast from the St. Paul Orpheum Theatre with Bert Parks and KSTP's Putnam, who later joined NBC radio in New York.

I remember Rex Stewart, Johnny Hodges, Ivy Anderson, and Herb Jeffries, and I recall Duke Ellington when he performed in the Coliseum Ballroom at Lexington and University in St. Paul. About the same time Les Brown and his big band enveloped the Club Casino of the Hotel St. Paul, broadcasting on KSTP radio and the NBC network.

Barnstorming, the Jimmy Lunceford band, on a one-nighter, blew the roof off the Eagles Hall in Minneapolis . . . Wham! Re-Bop-De-Boom-Bam! After hours, members of the Charlie Barnet Band jammed 'til dawn at another Clef Club, this one in Minneapolis, while bassist Oscar Pettiford sat in, later landing a long assignment that included playing Carnegie Hall with Duke Ellington.

At CBS-owned WCCO, a studio band preserved traditional and mainstream jazz in a weekly broadcast series arranged by Vince Bastien and featuring brother Biddy Bastien, formerly a bassist in the Gene Krupa Band in the days of Anita O'Day and Roy Eldridge.

I recall nationally recognized trumpeter and cornetist Paul "Doc" Evans, founder of Mendota's South Rampart Street Club and the Bloomington Symphony, transplanting the world of Bix Beiderbecke and Louis Armstrong for an audience sitting outdoors at Minneapolis's Walker Art Center.

Threepenny Opera memories! Ella Fitzgerald shook out a lead sheet prepared by singer-composer and Atlantic recording artist Patty McGovern, a St. Paul native, for a world-class takeoff on "Mack the Knife." The setting was Freddy's in downtown Minneapolis on Sixth Street. Three weeks later Ella went on to Berlin with the song, and jazz history was made when her manager, Norman Granz, recorded it for his Jazz at the Philharmonic series.

Musical events like these signaled a remarkable lowering of barriers for jazz. No longer did residents and visiting firemen swing, stomp, and listen only to country songs, polkas, and schottisches generated by Slim Jim, Whoopee John, the Six Fat Dutchmen, and Fezz Fritsche's Goose Town Band. No longer were ballroom, club, and concert venues reserved exclusively for opera, symphony, chamber music, and ballet buffs.

These days, a night on the town in the Twin Cities may offer a grand, concert-hall setting for jazz, such as Wynton Marsalis and the Lincoln Center Jazz Orchestra playing in Minneapolis's Orchestra Hall. Across the river, Billy Taylor and the Vocal Essence team produce a tribute to Martin Luther King at St. Paul's Ordway Center. In a more intimate setting, McCoy Tyner or Dave Brubeck appear at the University of Minnesota's Ted Mann Concert Hall.

In a truly intimate environment, where people *listen* to and *acknowledge* the music, artist Roy Haynes performs and records his tribute staged at Kenny Horst's Artists' Quarter in St. Paul. Back in Minneapolis at the Nicollet Mall's Dakota Jazz Club listeners can spend a night with Charles Lloyd or a new voice for jazz piano, Eldar Djangirov, compliments of club proprietor Lowell Pickett.

In St. Paul off Mears Park, Steve Heckler and his group spearhead a campaign for jazz during the annual Twin Cities Jazz Festival. In 2009 the journey from New Orleans to the headwaters of the Mississippi found Allen Toussaint, Esperanza Spalding, and Jon Weber headlining and broadcasting live on KBEM-FM (Jazz 88) from St. Paul's Lowertown. This is a *rich* jazz scene.

Now, with another barrier down, Twin Cities middle and high school students get exposure to the jazz experience. Curriculum and opportunities expand as students study musical scores, sight-read, improvise, and perform beyond the repertoire of the formal European orchestra, chamber groups, and marching bands. Students begin digging the world of improvisation and its jazz roots. Their inspirations are Duke Ellington, Louis Armstrong, Dizzy Gillespie, Miles Davis, Art Tatum, Teddy Wilson, Thelonious Monk, Stan Kenton, Benny Goodman, Oscar Peterson, and a host of others.

To the Twin Cities' jazz life, add this startling connection: live theater becomes a catalyst and messenger for *jazz language.* In 2009 St. Paul's internationally recognized Penumbra Theatre presented August Wilson's full plays, which are deeply rooted in jazz and the blues. Penumbra hosted *Joe Turner's Come and Gone,* the New York Drama Critics' Best Play of the Year, along with *The Piano Lesson,* winner of the 1990 Pulitzer Prize for Drama. Brendon Gill in the *New Yorker* called *Ma Rainey's Black Bottom,* "A genuine work of art."

The Twin Cities' jazz experience reflects a century-long jazz journey from the outflow to the headwaters of the Mississippi. Who knows how many hours musicians invested in creating and delivering and translating this music and its messages on the journey from New Orleans, where *some* of its roots were planted, by way of Kansas City, St. Louis, Chicago, New York, Los Angeles, San Francisco, Detroit, Cleveland, and other cities?

In *Joined at the Hip: A History of Jazz in the Twin Cities,* Jay Goetting documents—and stimulates—the geopolitical evolution of jazz, its audiences, and its artists from country roads to urban centers. To quote Edward Kennedy Ellington, the Duke, "The music, Jazz, is a call for Freedom!! Freedom!!!"

I invite you to read on!

Leigh Kamman
THE JAZZ IMAGE™

Introduction and Acknowledgments

Anyone who gets involved with jazz on a more-than-casual basis finds the music becomes an integral part of his or her existence. Jazz pervades the psyche. Jazz becomes an obsession.

Jazz players certainly know this. Serious listeners experience it. Writers, critics, and chroniclers of the art also know the feeling. I've been fortunate to fall into each of those categories over my lifetime. It was love of the music and an obvious unfilled need that led me to write this book.

About the time I retired as a reporter for the *Napa Valley Register,* I was visiting my native Twin Cities and reading *City of Gabriels,* Dennis Owsley's jazz history of St. Louis. In chatting with a good friend, pianist Ron Seaman, we noted there were published histories of the jazz scenes in the usual suspects—New Orleans, New York, Chicago, and Los Angeles, even Portland, Seattle, Detroit, and Memphis—but nothing for the Twin Cities.

With newfound time on my hands, a grasp of the craft of wordsmanship, and the jazz obsession, I launched this project. I sent questionnaires to dozens of musicians and those in the know, and then began interviewing key players. Seaman recalled that two fellows had started a similar project in the early 1990s. One of them, Dave Sletten, had met an untimely death from melanoma in 2000. The other, Kent Hazen, lacked time to take the book any further.

I contacted Dave's wife, Catharine Sletten, and after a sort of "job interview," she seemed pleased that someone was able to pick up the gauntlet. She gave my efforts her blessing. My initial meeting with Kent Hazen produced similar encouragement. They gave me full access to the boxes of clippings, notes, hundreds of hours of recorded—but largely untranscribed—interviews, and assorted memorabilia they had amassed. After Dave's death the materials had been housed at the Minnesota Historical Society in St. Paul.

With little written history of Twin Cities jazz available, the real treasure trove was the boxes of recordings and transcripts of dozens of interviews done mostly in the early and mid-1990s on KBEM radio by Dave and Kent for their series, *Twin Cities Jazz Remembered.* The informal single and group interviews, although occasionally imprecise, provide a wealth of material and emotional insight from some key players and observers of Twin Cities jazz, many of whom have since departed.

It is my hope that one day both the sound recordings and the transcripts, along with photographs and other material, will be publicly available in the archives of the Minnesota Historical Society and perhaps even at the Institute of Jazz Studies at Rutgers University in Newark, New Jersey, where assistant director Ed Berger was most helpful during my research visit. Both could serve as effective repositories for this valuable material.

Kent Hazen has become a real jazz friend, and he has continued to be "on call," reading my manuscript, offering editorial suggestions, and helping fact-check bits of history, names, and places. He has my sincere appreciation. Thanks also go to Jan Pearson, who meticulously and accurately transcribed many interviews.

While I've known radio personality Leigh Kamman for many years, this project brought us in touch regularly. Kamman has been active in the Twin Cities jazz world since the mid-twentieth century, and he has an encyclopedic knowledge of the jazz scene. I've enjoyed chatting with him and hearing that great voice, known to so many radio jazz fans over the years.

The folks at the Minnesota Historical Society Press have been a joy. And don't think I'm not really pleased to have a publisher excited about the project from day one. No knocking on doors with manuscript in hand. No letters of rejection. My original editor, Marilyn Ziebarth, got me off to a good start and ready for editor in chief Ann Regan, who has continued the encouragement. We all miss production manager Will Powers, who helped the book with format and graphics ideas and his more than passing fancy for the music we love before his sudden death in 2009.

Of course, thanks go to family and friends whom I believe understood when I said, "Sorry, can't do it . . . working on the book."

The full story of jazz's evolution in the Twin Cities—which paralleled national trends beginning with Dixieland early in the twentieth century and moving on to include swing in the thirties, bebop in the early forties, and later styles known variously as cool, avant-garde, progressive, and free jazz—would require an encyclopedic work. While I've done my best to fill these pages with the names, places, and events of jazz significance for the better part of a century, many invariably were missed or ended up on the proverbial cutting-room floor. For that I apologize, but I am also gratified that the Twin Cities has produced such a wealth of talent over the decades.

Joined at the Hip

1

Cruising Up the River

"In this bright future you can't forget your past."
—Bob Marley

It was a new sound. A different and exciting sound. Music that a person walking in downtown St. Paul before World War I had never heard before. It was a little like ragtime, a little like the old banjo-minstrel music, a bit like the brass-band music heard Sunday afternoons at the bandshell up the hill from the river. There was exuberance to it. Something that made a person near the steamboat landing quicken his step, even on a hot and humid July evening.

Wafting from the big sternwheeler at the Mississippi River landing at the foot of Jackson Street, which bustled until ice froze the river, came music that was brand new to these riverbanks. Jazz had stolen ashore, and it was quickly establishing a beachhead in the hearts and minds of curious Twin Cities residents.

Jazz didn't originate in St. Paul, of course. Nor did it necessarily even begin two thousand miles down the Mississippi in New Orleans, although it certainly had strong roots there. If jazz was already being played in St. Paul or its neighbor, Minneapolis, there is no record of this in the earliest years. And if jazz was born in the late nineteenth century, it was still in its infancy at the dawn of the twentieth.

In the beginning, jazz was a relatively simple music with multicultural origins. It was music that would have had an impact on people within earshot, and their reactions certainly would have been mixed: a combination

ST. PAUL LEVEE AND UNION DEPOT
Photo Copyright 1908 by T. W. Ingersoll.

The first jazz in the Twin Cities was likely heard near the foot of St. Paul's Jackson Street, where riverboats from as far south as New Orleans made their northernmost stop. Bix Beiderbecke and Louis Armstrong performed with these early bands.

of smiles, frowns, blank stares, and puzzled looks. New things are often greeted that way.

Minneapolis already boasted an opera house, art galleries, and a professional symphony orchestra, and both cities were noted for fondly supporting all manner of musical and artistic endeavors. So when that first hypothetical group of jazz musicians played there in the new twentieth century, the seeds they sowed fell on fertile ground.

Modern listeners transported back to this July day in the early 1900s might not recognize the music they heard as "jazz" since its parameters have evolved dramatically. The music played on the boats that traveled up and down the Mississippi and Ohio rivers was not strictly jazz of the improvised variety. Musicians inclined toward jazz had to sneak in its musical elements wherever and whenever they could. They might send little signals to one another and then subtly change the rhythm or judiciously insert improvised solos when they dared. Most riverboat bands probably

While St. Paul started out as more a jazz hub than its western neighbor, Minneapolis was growing, and its cosmopolitan atmosphere contributed to the growth of live music and jazz.

performed stock arrangements of popular songs preferred by the boats' operators.

Big riverboats had traveled up and down the Upper Mississippi since the middle of the nineteenth century. They had helped build important hubs of commerce and social activity in cities such as St. Louis, Davenport, Iowa, and even La Crosse, Wisconsin. It was in the latter where one large boat, the *J. S.*, burned to the waterline in 1910. The *J. S.*, built for excursions in 1901, was operated by the Streckfus brothers, who encouraged patrons to call it the *"Jess."* Some maintain that this boat nickname was the origination of the term *jazz*. Of course, pianist Jelly Roll Morton laid claim to having invented jazz music several years earlier. Morton, said music historian Irving Kolodin, rode a boat upriver to St. Paul in 1908.

Others assert that *jazz*, or the earlier spelling, *jass*, is a corruption of a term associated with sexual intercourse and that it dates to the early years when it entertained patrons in bordellos. In fact, although the word surfaced before the turn of the twentieth century, *jazz* was not a term in general use. Its first known appearance in a lyric was in the 1909 song

"Uncle Josh in Society," which included the line, "One lady asked me if I danced the jazz." In some circles it was treated like many other four-letter words—with disdain. *Etude Magazine* in 1924 noted, "If the truth were known about the origin of the word 'jazz,' it would never be mentioned in polite society."

Early jazz music was a hybrid of Western European, African, and Caribbean music synthesized and interpreted in great part by African American musicians. One jazz predecessor, ragtime, which "ragged" or syncopated the beat of popular marches, peaked shortly after the turn of the twentieth century with the music of Scott Joplin and others. Although it was notated music, it probably opened up some listeners' and players' ears to the possibility of experimentation and playing music off the page. But jazz's multiracial and multicultural origins probably stoked polite late-Victorian society to view it as an embarrassing bastard, even a threat to the purity of white culture and civilization.

Music heard on riverboats like the *J. S.* may have offered a respite from this rigidity. The *J. S.* and its sister ships were operated by the four Streckfus brothers, at least two of whom were musicians themselves. They often hand-picked their musicians. Among them was Fate Marable of Paducah, Kentucky, who ran the band on the *J. S.* beginning in 1907. Marable is often credited with bringing trumpeter Louis Armstrong aboard the riverboats, although John Streckfus likely ordered Marable to make the hire.

Louis Armstrong told New Orleans friends that in 1918 he planned to play on the steamer *Sidney* between New Orleans and Minneapolis. The following year, eighteen-year-old Armstrong probably saw the Twin Cities for the first time. This gave Twin Citians their first opportunity to hear a future jazz legend. Armstrong spent the better part of three years on riverboats but little time in St. Paul and Minneapolis, since he preferred the ambience of St. Louis, which later became his jumping-off point to Chicago and points east. An old-timer who played cornet in Weegee's Entertainers band downriver in Wabasha, Minnesota, said Armstrong played on excursion boats and "when the [riverboat] approached a town, the band would be out on the deck playing."

Many musicians including Armstrong, who called the riverboats his "university," learned to read music by playing stock arrangements of the "pretty" music that filled the boats' dance floors. But was this really jazz music? The Streckfus family, reflecting the era's traditions and racism,

Louis Armstrong (third from right) told New Orleans friends he would be heading up the river to Minneapolis when he joined the Fate Marable band in 1918. Aboard the SS *Capitol,* he and the other musicians mug for the camera: (left to right) Henry Kimball, Boyd Atkins, Marable, John St. Cyr, David Jones, Norman Mason, Armstrong, Norman Brashear, and "Baby" Dodds.

preferred genteel, broadly accepted music associated with danceable sounds, not the "hot" music the musicians played in New Orleans. The function of the riverboat bands was to please and entertain, not to proselytize this new style of music. That the latter actually happened was an unexpected and most beneficial side effect.

Early Minneapolis musician Tela Burt said in an interview that work for Twin Cities musicians on the boats was limited. Burt, a black saxophone player born in 1891 in Warrenton, North Carolina, moved to Minneapolis in 1912. The boats were good for some gigs, he said, and he "played a lot of those boat excursions on the Mississippi. But the big

A young Tela Burt came to the Twin Cities in 1912.

boats brought their own bands. They'd come up here and play and go back to New Orleans."

Most band members aboard the riverboats were African Americans. They rehearsed new music almost daily. Armstrong was the only one who soloed in Fate Marable's band on the steamer *Sidney*. Music historian Dennis Owsley in *City of Gabriels*, a jazz history of St. Louis, claims that "the romantic notion about jazz being played on the riverboats is false. There is little doubt, however, that the musicians did play jazz when they landed in cabarets and other halls."

Playing with Armstrong aboard the riverboat *Sidney* was Boyd Atkins, a musician born in New Orleans who later settled in Minneapolis for a time. Atkins played violin in Marable's aggregation and later became well known as an arranger and sax player at the Cotton Club and the El Patio (pronounced "PAY-show") in suburban Minneapolis. Playing with Atkins were then-local luminaries Lester Young, Rook Ganz, Harry Pettiford, and Adolphus Alsbrook.

Another famous jazz pioneer, influential cornetist Bix Beiderbecke, first heard jazz around the steamboat landings in his native Davenport, Iowa. Born in 1903, he came to the Twin Cities at least once during his short-lived career on the water. He was aboard the 228-foot *Majestic* during its last full year of operation, playing cornet and piano for just two weeks in 1921 with the Plantation Jazz Orchestra. The *Majestic* traveled an excursion route between Davenport and St. Paul but was consumed by fire in 1922. Beiderbecke opted for land-based engagements after that, joining the Ten Capitol Harmony Syncopators under the baton of Doc Wrixon. By this time St. Paul's steamboat landing was seeing greatly diminished commercial traffic because railroads, diesel-powered boats, and trucks were transporting goods more efficiently.

The pace of the dissemination of jazz across the land by live, in-person performances was necessarily slow. But the spread of jazz quickened after 1917, when the Original Dixieland Jass Band, a group of white New Orleans musicians, made the first popular jazz recordings, including "Indiana" and "Darktown Strutters' Ball" for the Victor Talking Machine Company. Jazz recordings quickly began bringing the new music from the waterfront into the parlor. Within a decade, radio arrived in people's homes, and with it broadcasts of dance band music. These new media combined to fan the embers of jazz into a full-blown wildfire.

In Minnesota's capital city, the skyscraping, twelve-story St. Paul Hotel, which had opened in 1910 on Rice Park above the river, started to become a major venue in the local music scene. El Herbert's band later made headlines when it was hired to perform there after the repeal of Prohibition, Herbert being one of the few black musicians to make a living playing in that era. (The Spanish Room on the hotel's second floor was the site of many remote broadcasts in the early days of radio's love affair with

While documentation of early "jazz" events is rare, this 1919 photograph of Frank Pallma's "Real 'Jazz' Band" was a harbinger of things to come. Personnel, left to right: Pete Bennetsen, Harry Anderson, Vic Blunck, Virgil Person, Frank Pallma, Ferd Oldre, Louis Garzon, H. Schreiber.

big bands playing swing music in the thirties and forties, and the hotel's Gopher Grill would play host to both local musicians and road bands.)

Musicians who came to the Twin Cities by riverboat occasionally stayed long enough for a short engagement at a number of local venues near the waterfront. Roy Robison, a native Minneapolitan whose parents were musical vaudevillians, recalled one of his earliest memories of hearing jazz in the cities. His father took Roy, who would become a prominent jazz saxophone player on the University of Minnesota campus in the early 1920s, to St. Paul to hear a jazz band perform in about 1914. "I knew what ragtime was," he said, "but this wasn't ragtime. This was jazz." Most likely this unidentified jazz band had arrived in St. Paul by steamboat.

While most players would have left for milder winters and more active music scenes, Minneapolis and St. Paul had began to grow their own and to attract players from elsewhere in the Upper Midwest. Robison vividly recalled hearing music at the Nankin Cafe in downtown Minneapolis during World War I. The band was "led by Jack Ermitinger, who was a fine banjoist. He had a band that could hardly be called Dixieland. Probably it was kind of a cross between Dixieland and ragtime. But they played well and they played a lot by ear, which wasn't too common."

Tela Burt, one of the first black musicians in the Twin Cities to enter the jazz realm, recalled that many of his colleagues got jobs as chauffeurs when only the rich had automobiles—and even those disappeared during the winter months: "They put the cars up at Thanksgiving and took them out again at Easter. [Minneapolis's] Nicollet Avenue was nothin' but sleds and horses." Burt, who lived at Twenty-seventh Avenue and Lake Street, regularly walked a long way to what would later become Minneapolis's center of after-hours jazz, the Near Northside. It was the site of the Black Elks club, where a Mrs. McCullough taught dancing and ran a five-piece orchestra which prompted Burt's short-lived musical career.

Burt worked at Minneapolis's Odin Club, a gathering place for wealthy Scandinavians on Second Avenue and Sixth Street in a bank building. Prior to a stint in the army, Burt "went to work as a porter and I worked up to be bartender. Then they made me head bellman, and the next year they made me assistant manager. They called me the 'smoked Swede' cause I knew all the drink orders in Swedish."

During World War I, Burt found himself in France as a supply sergeant who was responsible for ninety-eight band instruments. Only some were being used, so he began puttering with the saxophone. When he returned to the Twin Cities, he studied at MacPhail School of Music and took saxophone lessons from Chester Groth (before Groth established his well-known downtown Minneapolis music store). Burt began playing professionally around 1920. He called the sax "a clown instrument" but admired one of the top players of the day, Rudy Wiedoeft. Burt said that when Wiedoeft "played the sax, you thought it was a cello. I used to practice my tone from him. I got every record I could when he was playing." Roy Robison recalled that Wiedoeft was his father's friend: "When I was a kid, Rudy sent me an autographed picture and wished me well. I used to play one of his saxophone solos, maybe 'Saxophobia.' Later, I got to think of them as sort of old hat and corny. They were written saxophone solos."

Bass player Dave Faison, who knew Tela Burt in the early thirties, recalled a number of musicians who traveled up the Mississippi to the Twin Cities. The players on one steamer included Chet Gould on bass, Paul Cooper on piano, Stan Fritz on trombone, Nels Laxal on trumpet, Kenny Driscoll on drums, and Pappy Trester. All were considered good

Tela Burt, at 103, shows off musical memorabilia dating back nearly seventy-five years. He was interviewed in his Minneapolis home by Dave Sletten and Kent Hazen in 1994. He died the following year.

Dixieland musicians, but Faison added that they could vary their styles: "They used to do land office business every night . . . Before Spike Jones was ever known, the Twin Cities was the novelty band capital." Vic Sell was one of the riverboat musicians. Fate Marable, who was aboard the riverboat *Sidney* around 1919, would spend summers on the Upper Mississippi. Later, in 1937 when Freddie Fisher and his Schnickelfritz Band "came up from Winona . . . and was discovered by Rudee Vallee's agent at the Midway Gardens, it got him in a couple of movies."

Lawyer Ken Green, who was a pianist of some repute when boogie-woogie was becoming popular on the University of Minnesota campus, recalled hearing the song "Darkness on the Delta" in 1933 emanating from the *Capitol* steamer docked in St. Paul: "You'd go down to the foot of Jackson Street from downtown St. Paul, much the same as it still is. The boat would have cruises in the afternoon and at night . . . In a way it was a god-awful trip because of the sewage in the Mississippi River . . . You went by South St. Paul where the smell of those packing plants was frightful. You stayed inside." He remembered mostly, though, being "very excited because they had this black band on there, and I thought it was going to be Louis Armstrong. I was disappointed it wasn't Armstrong, but these guys were *good*."

2

Jazz, Jazz Everywhere—and Not a Drop to Drink

"Suddenly there's work. There's tons of work for jazz musicians. Prohibition is loosening up morals. It's doing exactly the opposite of what it was supposed to do."
—Gary Giddins, *critic and writer*

In 1920, St. Paul author F. Scott Fitzgerald had just completed writing *This Side of Paradise,* a touchstone novel that came to symbolize the post–World War I flapper-and-jazz generation. In January of the same year, the Eighteenth Amendment to the U.S. Constitution outlawed alcohol in the United States. Its congressional sponsor was Andrew Volstead, a Republican congressman from Minnesota (who reportedly consumed a pound of chewing tobacco every day).

During the "Noble Experiment" legislating liquor consumption, alcohol went underground. Drinks became not impossible to get, just more difficult—depending on whom you knew and where you were. And jazz followed alcohol underground. Despite the clandestine nature of the music and its performance venues, what emerged came to be known as "The Jazz Age." According to Fitzgerald, during Prohibition, "the parties were bigger . . . the pace was faster . . . and the morals were looser." Jazz and "jazzy" music became the popular music of the day—a phenomenon that would last into the so-called "Swing Era" of the thirties, through Prohibition's repeal in 1933, and on into the forties.

In the Twin Cities during Prohibition, speakeasies, after-hours joints, and "private" clubs serving liquor and playing jazz opened their doors and blossomed.

Even though alcohol was rarely served in many ballrooms and larger establishments before alcohol was outlawed, the legal ban seemed to tempt owners to bend the law. Saxophonist Frankie Roberts said, "There was no difference between then and now. People brought their own and bought setups. Speakeasies were not as classy as the hotels and clubs. You bought liquor from the speakeasies."

Roberts often played for gangsters and underworld figures: "There was an all-night place in St. Paul—Chicago hoodlums used to come there when the heat was on them. We'd go up there several nights a week and just play for tips. They'd say, 'Hey, play "Melancholy Baby,"' and lay a sawbuck on us, y'know?" Violence could be part of the burgeoning underworld, and at one downtown speakeasy, Roberts "saw a sawed-off shotgun and thought the minute he moves toward it, I'm climbing over the upright piano... There were some pretty tough boys there. There were shootings. They found some of those boys in the alley."

Nettie Hayes Sherman, who played piano at the speakeasy Than's in downtown St. Paul in the 1920s, said syndicate members were well-dressed and good tippers: "The Chicago mob was active in St. Paul... and Than's was a powerhouse. It was the place to go to be with people who were well known in St. Paul. Than was a protector of the mob. There was a house rule that no one was to be called by their name, so it was safe for frequenters such as Tommy O'Connell, John Dillinger, Baby Face Nelson, and so many others." She recalled that Nelson had an eye for her. One night she was "being tormented by a black customer. The man yelled to me, 'Honey, can you play "Shortnin' Bread"?' Baby Face Nelson walked up behind the man, picked him up by his shirt collar, and threw him onto the street." Not long after, Baby Face proposed to her. "Of course I told the man no," Sherman said.

The syndicate, she said, "used to come to St. Paul, which they called the 'City of the Lam(b)s,' after pulling a job... They would stay at a mansion on White Bear Lake, and at night they would come out and head for Than's. They mingled with the crowd and no one knew the better for it... Those gangsters looked just like anyone else. They dressed in very fine suits and hats. They looked like businessmen. John Dillinger, for example...

Frankie Roberts, born in 1905, was coming into his own musically when the Roaring Twenties and Prohibition were at their peak. Playing for underworld figures was commonplace. He eventually became one of the most in-demand musicians to hail from the Twin Cities.

You just wouldn't know they were gangsters unless you got to know them and they trusted you."

Isadore Blumenfeld, who became known as "Kid Cann," grew up at Sixteenth and Franklin avenues in Minneapolis. He had at least three nightspots on the city's Near Northside. Most nightclubs and after-hours places were "key clubs" with strictly controlled memberships. Tela Burt recalled that the "key clubs were nothin' but millionaire clubs where guys brought their secretaries . . . and those guys had all the liquor you could think of. They even played roulette out there, had gambling and everything." Burt said that in Excelsior on Lake Minnetonka, just west of Minneapolis, "They had a policeman at the gate, and they had one when you entered the place. Nobody could get in unless he was a key member." Burt said he'd "play all night on Saturday nights. I'd come back with thirty or forty dollars in my pocket Sunday morning. And they had a whole gang of them places. They had one down there in South St. Paul. They had another one about twenty miles south of St. Paul."

Burt also played music at Kid Cann's establishments on the Near Northside, though Burt recalled, "We just called it 'Sixth and Lyndale North,' that's all . . . Downstairs they had a luncheon, and upstairs they had the dance hall. Cann used to come and sit right in front of the orchestra. He used to give us tips. He had a lot of money." Kid Cann later ran operations from his Flame Night Club and Cafe headquarters at 1523 Nicollet Avenue (later known as Club Carnival). By 1942, the FBI had tagged Cann as "the overlord of the Minneapolis underworld." Pianist and vocalist Jeanne Arland Peterson, matriarch of one of the Twin Cities' premier music families, met Kid Cann when she was starting out in the late 1930s.

Although little evidence exists to substantiate the claim by newspaperman Walter Liggett that Governor Floyd B. Olson's administration had ties to Kid Cann and other gangsters, Nettie Sherman recalled a strange meeting between Olson and Baby Face Nelson: "Floyd was sitting in a booth when Baby Face joined him . . . I watched the two of them talking for about two or three hours about lord knows what . . . Neither one had the slightest idea who he was talking to." In 1935 Liggett was gunned down, allegedly by Cann, who was never convicted of the murder. Ironically, the busy thoroughfare that crosses Sixth and Lyndale North is known as Floyd B. Olson Memorial Highway.

Downtown St. Paul hosted another popular club of the time, the Green Lantern, where Red Dougherty played piano. Red recalled that John Dillinger might place a hundred-dollar bill on the piano in the company of Baby Face Nelson. Nelson, according to Red, played twenties-style ragtime and bar room piano. Drummer and vibraharpist Eddie Tolck played the Green Lantern with Dougherty and Chief McElroy on drums. Tolck described the venue as a place "where gangsters hung out," including, on occasion, Al Capone. "They'd sit in a booth and divvy up money and sometimes deal with the St. Paul police. Gangsters didn't bother the general populace," said Tolck. "All the violence was within themselves."

St. Paul was known as a safe city for gangsters during the 1930s. Journalist Susan Berman, who chronicled the activities of her gangster-father, Davie Berman, wrote in *Easy Street*, "For bribes of thirty-five dollars and upwards, and a promise not to commit any crimes within a fifty-mile radius of the city, the gangsters were safe. The police would look the other way."

Prior to Mayor Hubert Humphrey's city cleanup in the 1940s, Minneapolis officials were also known for looking the other way where mobsters were concerned. After-hours gambling clubs were everywhere, many of them featuring local musicians playing jazz. The "class" locations of the day had their share of underworld activity, too. Davie Berman was said to have operated his racing book out of a second-floor "office" at the Radisson Hotel and later at the Dyckman Hotel. Kid Cann owned the Williams Bar, where cornetist Doc Evans later played, and was said to have come in once a week to check the books with gangster Lucky Luciano at his side.

Player Roy Robison said that during Prohibition, "there was a lot of drinking, of course... and inevitably a bootlegger outside when you went in. He sold moonshine to whoever went by. I was standing out there during intermission, when somebody inquired about getting some moonshine and asked, 'Is it any good?' The dealer pointed to somebody laid out on the car seat and said, 'Is it any good? He was drinking it.' Out cold." (Drugs, Robison said, were relatively uncommon, although by the thirties, marijuana may have been making an appearance.) Robison said Curly Shapiro, who owned and ran the thriving after-hours spot Curly's at Sixth and Hennepin, wore a tuxedo and went "legit" after the amendment was repealed. When authorities "finally started to enforce after-hours drinking... Curly had the bright idea of serving drinks in coffee cups. You would come in at 1:30 at Curly's, and here would be all these people sitting around drinking liquor but it seemed like they were drinking coffee." (Curly's later become the House of Hastings Restaurant, then Jimmy Hegg's Starlight Club, before it burned down in 1958.)

During the 1920s Tela Burt's calendar stayed full: "I'd have two or three gigs every weekend. There was no radio or nothin'. People didn't hear any music, see, and you could take five numbers and play them for a year, and nobody ever wondered what was happening. But when radio come out in 1921 or '22 and they started hearing these new pieces, they started asking you to play this and play that. The first four or five years when I had my orchestra, I had a repertoire of about fifteen pieces. And when I quit, in 1934, I had a repertoire of about forty." Burt called himself a "mechanical musician." He and his bandmates read from scores and did not improvise.

Hotels in St. Paul and Minneapolis provided opportunities for men like Burt to work musically, and otherwise. Blacks dominated the porter, bellman, and kitchen posts. Unusual for the period, Burt played Minneapolis's Leamington Hotel at a time when most of the players were white. While the music Burt and others played in clubs and hotels might not have been true jazz, it was certainly "jazzy," and it was laying the groundwork for more improvisational sounds to come.

In these early years, jazz was primarily dance music, not "concert" music for listening. Dance halls provided a home for larger musical groups, such as one called the Arcadia (also known as the Track). Burt said, "Maybe two or three times a year I'd have a big band. I'd get that dance hall in front of the courthouse. I'd have twelve or fourteen pieces. We never played over five men in the clubs, but down at the dancing school we had eight—they called it the Palms, at 242 Nicollet and right on the corner, upstairs. Women were available to dance with customers at ten cents a dance. A fellow named Stocking ran the place—I played there from 1924 to '28 . . . four nights a week. That was called a practice dance. And that was open to men only. The girls received two and a half cents of the ten."

Art Landry's Curtis Hotel Orchestra is often credited with bringing dancing to the Minneapolis club and restaurant scene in 1919. Landry's was also said to be the first Minneapolis orchestra to record commercially, initially on the Gennett label and later for the Victor Talking Machine

Company. Few, if any, of the musicians in these recording bands were Minnesotans. Landry left the Twin Cities alone to seek his fortune back east, where he formed new bands, some of whose early recordings have survived.

One important Twin Cities venue, the Marigold Gardens (later Ballroom), began its long life in 1919 on Nicollet Avenue between Thirteenth and Grant. The spot became so popular in the 1920s and 1930s that Nicollet streetcars stopped directly in front—in the middle of the block—to let off dancers. The Marigold's prominent sign promised, "Never Grow Old Dancing at the Marigold." Big names played there, while local bands like Cece Hurst and Norvy Mulligan kept the regulars coming back for more. Over the years some three hundred "Cupid Club" couples who met at the room danced all the way to the altar.

In the 1920s Tela Burt played several times at the Marigold, which was by far the largest hall around. He also played at Minneapolis's South Side Club, on Twelfth Avenue at Third Street, on Monday nights. Burt's favorite player to call for work was Sidney Williams, whom he described as "the best piano player I guess Minnesota ever produced. He wrote music and played, and he had a studio in Minneapolis. He was the first guy I ever played with." Williams recorded several impressive two-fisted solo piano sides for Victor Records in the early 1930s.

Another pianist with Burt, Clarence Johnson, had a hard time because he was unable to read music. "He couldn't read note one, but if he heard a piece he could sit down and play," Burt explained. Johnson "formed a band here called the 'Shortnecks.' None of them could read music, and brother, they could play. From the 1920s up until the '30s, they had about six or seven pieces, but normally if you couldn't read, you didn't play with us. See, you had to read."

Other popular early Twin Cities ballrooms included the Arcadia in Minneapolis, across from the courthouse on Fifth Street. In St. Paul, the Coliseum Ballroom, owned by John Lane and adjacent to Lane's Boulevards of Paris, one of the cities' finest nightclubs, was located at University and Lexington. The Coliseum, built as an ice rink in 1918, was known for music at all hours of the day and night. When it eventually met its demise, a portion of the building was used for the left-field wall at Lexington Park, home of the St. Paul Saints baseball club.

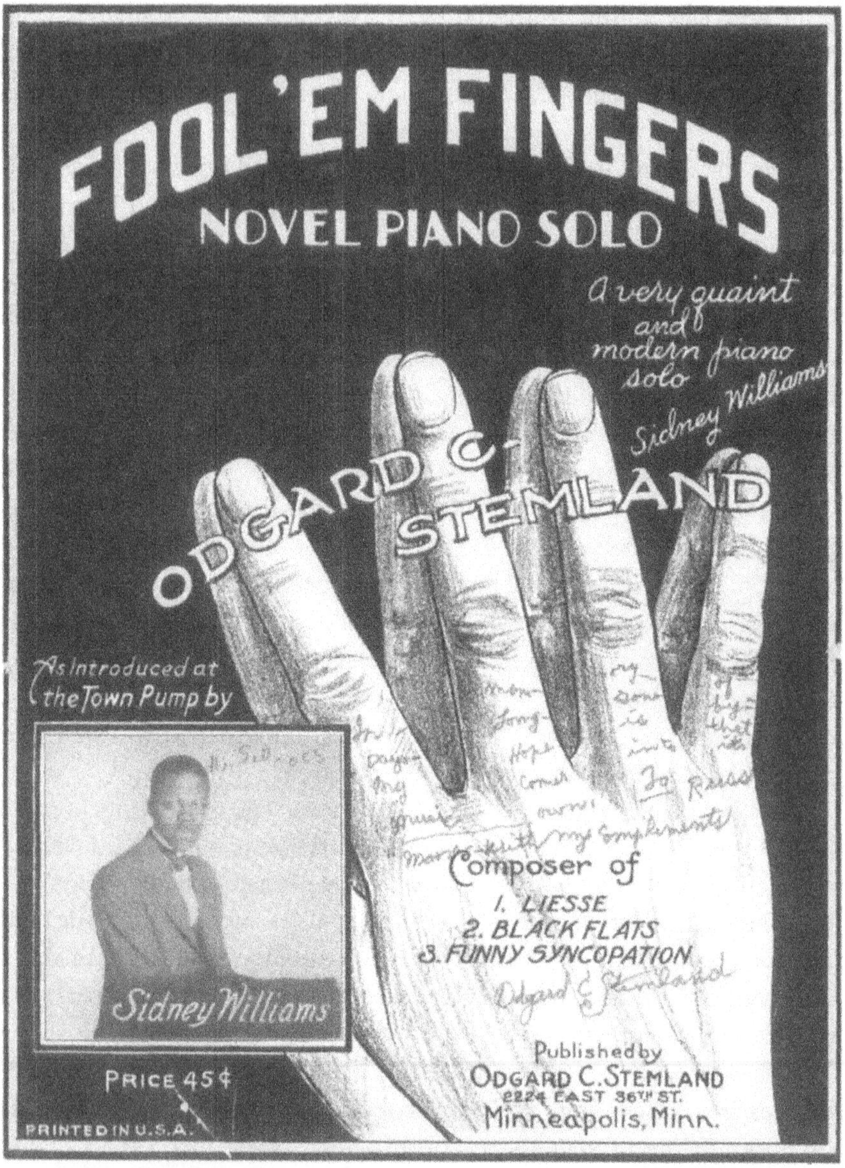

Sid Williams, a highly regarded keyboard artist in the 1920s, recorded for Victor Records and ran St. Paul's Como Theater, which opened in 1926 "with colored management."

Red Maddock fronted the Lloyd Cowden Band at the Trianon Ballroom, at Nicollet and Lake in Minneapolis, in 1933. Another Trianon venue was located south of the Twin Cities. Left to right: Arne Gilbertson, piano; Wally Schultz, basses; Sam Giltner, guitar; Buzz Nelson, drums; front row: saxes, Marv Wells, Bud Pike, Lloyd Cowden; back row: Barney Bakula, trumpet; Franklyn Miller, trumpet; Harold Moer, trombone; Ryan "Dutch" Fries, trombone; George "Red" Maddock, dancer and vocals.

Lesser-known Twin Cities ballrooms during Prohibition and in the 1930s included the Oxford on Selby in St. Paul, the Trianon south of the cities, and the Eagle Lake Pavilion northwest of Minneapolis near Osseo. Major hotels also had large rooms with dance floors that they called "ballrooms," and dance pavilions popped up at Lake Minnetonka, Excelsior, and White Bear Lake north of St. Paul. Even the Crystal Ballroom in Fargo, North Dakota, was known in the Twin Cities. Duke Ellington's Orchestra made a well-known live recording there in 1940 that included such Ellington standards as "Mooche," "Ko-Ko," and "Mood Indigo." Sid Williams ran the Como Theater in St. Paul, which opened in 1926 "with colored management." On the bill were Reginald Denny in *Rolling Home,* along with dancers Whiting and Willis, the "Masters of Syncopation." Jane Green was listed as a top jazz vocalist singing "The Blues."

Tela Burt recalled other musicians from the twenties including the Curry boys, Paul on violin and Charles on trumpet. They were members of Burt's band called the Unique Syncopators. The brothers' sister, Nelly Curry, sang. George True, who eventually left the Twin Cities for Seattle, was the band's drummer, and player Bill Moore moved to Canada. "I used to do bookings, and I had fifty or sixty musicians to book on my list," said

Burt. "About four or five were white. I always had a mix in my band. I had a sousaphone player; he was white. I had a trumpet player; he said he had Negro blood in him, but nobody would believe it if you claimed you had Negro blood. But he was one of the best trumpet players in town. I had him for about three or four years. And that guy, he couldn't play unless he had half a pint of liquor in him, but he could play more trumpet than you ever heard. We called him 'Red.' He had red hair."

Burt felt he had to keep the fact that he played jazz concealed from his family because his father, a minister, didn't approve. Burt did not associate much with other players off the bandstand, and his colleagues who made their living playing were often hard drinkers and carousers. Burt gave up playing in 1934 and married his second wife, Edythe Smith, in 1940. He claimed that Duke Ellington married her sister (historical accounts refute this). Burt said, "Duke used to come here whenever he'd play, he'd come over to my house. If I had still been playing, he would have taken me into his orchestra." Burt, who eventually had some success in real estate, organized marching bands and baseball teams and was active in the Johnny Baker Post of the American Legion before his death in 1995 at age 104.

In the years when Burt's bookings were at their peak, fraternities and sororities at the University of Minnesota helped provide occasions for would-be musicians to develop their skills. Burt remembered at least a half dozen parties each weekend. Musicians welcomed jobs playing for Greek-society rushes, "sunlight hops," and post-game socials, as well as the proms, balls, and formal affairs that usually called for bands of twelve pieces or more. Campus homecoming festivities were a bigger opportunity than New Year's Eve.

Besides the professionals who played for these events, the campus hosted many student bands and orchestras. Even prior to 1920, the *Minnesota Daily* student newspaper listed such groups as the Casey Red Campus Dance Orchestra, Rawhide Murphy's Stupendous Orchestra, the Campus Syncopaters, and the Minnesota Glee Club Jazz Band.

While the University of Minnesota campus was considered a hotbed of evolving jazz music in the Twin Cities, student musicians did not join the musicians' union. Union members were typically older, and they depended on playing more conservative styles of music to make their living.

Players often resented and felt threatened by the upstart new music that was turning the heads of the young people. Campus musicians apparently looked down their noses at the stodgier men in the American Federation of Musicians. Bad blood between the two factions was common and even tangible. Saxophonist Roy Robison said, "Those stooges that played down in the theaters, there was a certain snobbery really. They looked down on us."

Robison said his clique of campus musicians didn't actually play jazz: "It wasn't jazz at all. It was just pop music . . . and we didn't refer to any of the campus bands as jazz bands." Robison's "first exposure" to jazz was probably hearing Paul Wilke's Orchestra, "a very fine campus band. That was probably in 1922 . . . A guy named [Kenny] Kramer was the trumpet player. They played somewhat of a Dixieland style, I suppose, or rather a campus style." Reflecting back, he said, "I think there really was a University of Minnesota campus style. For instance, what Doc Evans was playing later was really Dixieland. But the style of music played on the campus in the mid-twenties was pop music and a lot of ballads, just the pop songs of the day." (Robison also remembered that Ben Pollack's band was "the best band that ever played regularly in the Twin Cities." Pollack later used one of Robison's tunes, "In the Evening," as a theme song.)

Newspaperman Russ Roth wrote in the *Minneapolis Tribune* years later that the university campus was the center of jazz activities in the Twin Cities throughout the twenties. The two most popular groups were Norvy Mulligan's and Fatso Palmer's bands. The Palmer band, headed by Paul Wilke until 1927, like most others, went to Stiffy's, a campus hangout, to listen to Red Nichols recordings. Stiffy Steadman's Gopher and Joe Crane's Bookstore in Dinkytown became places where students and campus musicians congregated to listen to Nichols, Duke Ellington, and Ben Pollack. They would copy different things from records. Even when they had to play the smooth, pretty tunes, they would use their newly borrowed licks when they gathered to play jazz for themselves. Roth wrote, "Everyone agrees that Red Nichols' early records had the greatest influence on the course that campus Dixieland took. Much of this may have been owing to the fact that Palmer attended Culver military academy in the early twenties, where he was Nichols' roommate." It's no secret that Nichols recorded more prolifically than Beiderbecke and that Nichols's records were marketed more aggressively.

Musician and historian Carl Warmington recalled the "ultimate competition" between bands on campus. Two top groups, with at least a dozen players each, would stage a "Battle of Music." That gave way to the "cutting contests," which gave individual players the chance to show their stuff. Warmington said after these events, dancers and musicians alike would head for Child's Restaurant on Nicollet Avenue, a popular spot for late-night pancakes in the early twenties. After it closed, the Rainbow Cafe on Hennepin and Lake Street became the place to go.

Instrumentation in campus bands ranged from three to eight pieces, depending on a fraternity's or sorority's music budget. The clarinet became popular as a doubling instrument for the saxophonist and increased the Dixieland flavor. The piano, drums, banjo or guitar, and bass, which could be a bass sax, tuba, string bass, or sousaphone, carried the rhythmic pulse. The two-beat rhythm gradually moved to four and produced a happier, more spirited brand of jazz. The horns usually played as an ensemble during the first chorus; the clarinet or sax, trumpet, and trombone followed with a chorus in that order, sometimes two or three choruses, if the spirit moved. All horns would join in the final "out-chorus."

Warmington played with Paul Wilke's Campus Band in the summer of 1922 on a launch, owned by Richard Putnam, that ferried groups around Lake Minnetonka. Warmington reminisced about some of the era's popular tunes: "What exciting sounds floated across the lake as we waited in the launch for the one o'clock wind-up. Wilke's Band played the popular tunes of the day, 'Ja-Da,' 'China Boy,' 'The Sheik,' and 'Carolina in the Morning,' but the most repeated selection was a new tune from the Broadway show *Shuffle Along* called 'Running Wild.' Over and over this song was played—encore after encore. The spirited tempo and the fascinating rhythm still bounces around in my memory after many decades. The Jazz Age was in full swing."

John Marshall Palmer, who later became a Minneapolis attorney, had another popular band in the era. Roy Robison called Palmer "the greatest cornet player, next to Bix, that I have ever heard." Palmer's band featured him playing cornet, Jack Daniels on clarinet and sax, Art Goldberg on piano, Mel Wright on guitar, and Dwight Hammond on drums. Robison later took Daniels's place on sax, while Gordie Bowen played bass sax whenever a job called for a six-piece band. "We couldn't find a trombone player on campus who could play jazz," Palmer said. "We had to make the bass sax do as a substitute. Our music was all instrumental. No singing. Goldberg was a magnificent pianist... He couldn't read a note when he started with us. But we seldom, if ever, used music anyway." It is especially high praise that the all-black union of domestic servants hired the Palmer band to play for its annual ball one year.

By the time Goldberg left the Twin Cities for Hollywood in 1934, he had established himself as one of the top keyboardists around. After going west, he adopted the professional name Arthur Morton. He had studied cello as a child, but when his mother prodded him to practice, he said, "I'd rather listen to Paul Whiteman." Morton also cited Bix, Sam Lanin, and Boots Matern and his Musical Monkeys as influences. Years later, Morton compared the Twin Cities favorably with other centers of music around the country. Minneapolis had "the symphony. As far as I was concerned, it was the most. It was a wonderful time of my life; whether for jazz or classical [music], I was a lucky man to have grown up in Minneapolis."

The music action in downtown Minneapolis began picking up as the city's population edged up to almost 400,000. Among its popular venues were the modern Radisson Hotel, completed in 1909 between Seventh and Eighth streets by Simon and Edna Dickerson Kruse and labeled by the *Minneapolis Journal* "the last word in hotel perfection." It offered good music for patrons as long as the Kruses ran it (until 1934). Nearby were two vaudeville houses, the Orpheum and the Miles Theater (later known as the Century).

The Radisson's first major dining and entertainment space was the Chateau Room, which featured a quintet of Minneapolis Symphony Orchestra musicians. In 1925 Kruse installed an unusual moveable bandstand on rollers in the new Flame Room, the first of three by that name. The room could be reduced to accommodate one hundred diners or expanded to allow six hundred dancers. Craig Buie was a trumpet player in the Flame Room band fronted by Slatz Randall during the 1920s. He had spent a good deal of time on the road and aboard cruise ships, but when they played in Milwaukee, they got to know a dance team on the Orpheum circuit. The dancers often stayed at the Radisson in Minneapolis, and Buie asked them to help the band get a booking. It worked. "In a short time, we were filling the room on Saturday nights with almost no advertising," Buie said.

Randall was a native of Little Falls, Minnesota, who played piano for Hal Kemp's first band formed at the University of North Carolina, known as the Carolina Club Orchestra. Randall's first band also took on the Carolina Club name. He traveled extensively before returning to the Twin Cities in 1929. Among the Randall sidemen was Ish Jones, a good arranger and "take-off man" on sax, later replaced by Gordie Bowen. Buie recounted an experience from 1929: "Columbia would send out recording units to record some of the Minnesota ethnic bands playing polkas. One of the unit managers stopped in and suggested that we make a trial record of [the more jazz-oriented] 'Bessie Couldn't Help It.' Joe Roberts, our singer and banjo player, really would shine on that tune. Joe was a pretty good banjo and guitar player. He didn't read music, but he knew the standard tunes. He was very placid when he was playing and looked half asleep." Buie said, "Most jazz band directors were not good musicians, but they were good businessmen. Joe was not able to take advantage of his opportunity as a bandleader, but he was brilliant when he was selling a song." Musician and historian Dick Raichelson described Roberts's style as "high strung." Roberts, who finally did lead his own band and became a Broadway producer, dressed in a waiter's uniform when he sang.

Columbia made at least a half dozen recordings of the Slatz Randall band in 1929 and 1930 in Minneapolis for its Brunswick label. The Randall band played the Radisson until just before the stock market crash of 1929, and the group managed to stay together until 1937. "There were some mighty fine musicians in Minneapolis during those years," said Buie. "We recruited them when we had sickness or resignations from our band."

Local jazz scenes are microcosms of the world jazz scene, with good, bad, mediocre, and outstanding players, but some talent pools are bigger and deeper than others. Compared to other metropolitan areas of similar size, the Twin Cities always ranked favorably, enjoying the reputation of being a good place for traveling bands to pick up top-notch sidemen. Roy Robison recalled the "great number of good musicians in Minneapolis during the twenties and thirties, particularly. There were very fine musicians here. Many of them later went on and had careers in New York playing for bigger bands."

Craig Buie's own reputation was that of a hard-swinging trumpet player, and he played a long time, well into his eighties. He said, "Doc Van Deusen, the trombone player, paid me a compliment. He said a fellow came up to him and said, 'This guy Buie has more drive than any trumpet player in town.'"

Also playing at the Flame Room for a half dozen years beginning in 1931 was Norvy Mulligan's band. KSTP radio regularly featured the Flame Room on *Dancing in the Twin Cities,* its performers sharing the spotlight with the St. Paul Hotel band. Mulligan's twelve-piece band also played at the Coconut Grove at Sixth and Hennepin above Schinder's newsstand. Coconut Grove was a club frequented by gangsters, according to Raichelson.

One of the "mighty fine musicians" mentioned by Buie was Frankie Roberts. As a teenager in Albion, Nebraska, Roberts performed in a community band that sent off soldiers as they boarded trains during World War I and sometimes played for funerals of fallen soldiers. In 1917 the jazz bug bit him when he was standing outside his hometown drug store and heard the "Original Dixieland One-Step," by the Original Dixieland Jazz Band. The drug store sold phonographs, and the record had been provided for demonstration purposes. "It was the first time I'd ever heard anything like that. That really turned me on," Roberts remembered. Roberts tried to imitate Larry Shields, the clarinetist with the Original Dixieland Jazz Band, and by 1919 Roberts had formed a small jazz-oriented group: "We were probably pretty bad. The soldiers were home, and everybody wanted to dance. We'd go out and make all of five dollars each."

The group left Nebraska in 1922 as McDonald's Novelty Five. Roberts was billed as the "Saxophone Shark" and the "Clarinet Wizard." The band first traveled in a Packard twin-six auto that would always overheat. In October 1924 the band drove up to Minneapolis from Omaha in a Model T: "We couldn't figure out how to get downtown. We had heard that everyone spoke Swedish and the kids went to school on snowshoes. We saw a milk wagon and asked directions. We could hardly understand him."

After six months of playing at the Marigold Ballroom, Roberts's band was replaced by the New Orleans Rhythm Kings, a famous recording and touring band of white New Orleans musicians who influenced a generation of players in the Twin Cities and many other places where they performed. Roberts remembers that this Rhythm Kings engagement, which lasted several months, was a true watershed event for the Twin Cities jazz scene. All the local jazzers spent as much time at the Marigold as possible. Roberts claimed that local bands played a lot differently after this gig than they had before it. Other veterans who were there concurred with

Les Beigel's Dixieland group was one of the most popular around in the mid-thirties: Hal Runyon on trombone; Biddy Bastien, bass; Frankie Roberts, clarinet; Chief McElroy, drums; Beigel; and unknown, piano.

this assessment. Roy Robison said they weren't yet eighteen, the legal age to get in to the Marigold: "Art Goldberg and I would stand out in the alley and listen to them. We'd get a soapbox or something and stand up right by the window where the bandstand was and listen to them."

It was 1925, and radio had not yet fully caught on, so Roberts's bandleader bought a music store in Wayzata and turned it into a dance hall. The band went on the road again but eventually was booked at the Radisson, then back to the Marigold. About that time, Frankie Roberts and bassist Biddy Bastien went to see Ben Pollack's band at the Nicollet Hotel. Pollack wanted Roberts to go on the road with him. "Don't you want to get your name in *DownBeat?*" he asked the young reed man. Frankie turned him down since he was getting all the work he could handle close to home. Then, in 1937, Frankie Roberts and Craig Buie hooked up. Roberts "was a top clarinetist," said Buie. "The band at Lindy's [Fourth and Hennepin] was one of the bands that I recall. Les Beigel, Hal Runyon, and Frankie Roberts made up the front line. Randall thought Runyon was the best trombone player he had ever heard. Les had been there quite a while, and he was going to play in Chicago, so their band was breaking up. When I walked in, they booked me with a small band. I hired Jack Christy on piano. He was a great pianist, but quite a character."

Les Beigel, who had gone to Chicago, wanted to return to the Twin Cities. "I wrote to Frankie Roberts, Biddy Bastien, and Hal Runyon in July or August that I wanted to go back. Gus [Arnheim] was going to the coast, and I didn't want to go," said Beigel. "I think Jack Malerich was instrumental in talking to the fellows at Lindy's Café about putting together a Dixieland band. We had jammed so many times together."

It was at Lindy's that Beigel met Glenn Miller for the second time. (The first was back in Omaha in 1926 when Miller was touring with Ben Pollack's band.) This time Miller had his own band at the Nicollet Hotel, and band members would come around to Lindy's when they finished their hotel gig at 12:30 AM. "After midnight, we would have a jam session. Then Glenn said, 'This town is not big enough for you. You've got to join my band.'"

Beigel did a stint with the Miller band, but he remained a Dixielander at heart. He wrote an article for *DownBeat* that described Dixieland as "an American art form" with three important ingredients: "1. Improvisation—that means it is unrestrained by the written part. You may have a written part, but the player is not supposed to just sit there and read the notes as they are written—it allows for individual interpretation. 2. Syncopated rhythms—the drummers don't just play band-style drums. You need individuality in the drummer. Accenting the offbeat mainly is what made the rhythm. When the brass band would go 'one-dum-bom-bom,' and you hear them 'chut-and-chut-and chut-and chut.' 3. Contrapuntal ensemble playing—two or more contrasting melody lines that complement each other." When Roy Robison later compared musical genres, he contrasted rock and roll's "manufactured excitement" with Dixieland's "normal and real excitement." Dixieland was "not a music of just teenage kids. It appealed to young adults as well, and even more." Good dance or pop bands of that time made records, he noted, that "sold to everyone from fourteen to forty or eighty."

Beigel recalled fondly his days with Red Nichols. The auspicious beginning with the famed cornetist and bandleader came in 1933 at the height of the Great Depression, when President Roosevelt closed the banks. Nichols had to pay his sidemen with IOUs. When Beigel needed a tuxedo, Nichols dug deep into his trunk and found him an outfit. He also supplied Beigel with a "new" Bach trumpet. Beigel recalled, "When I came on the job, I was feeling bad. They were really sad days. Then I saw the trumpet and said, 'What's this?' He said, 'Try it. If you like it, use it.' I carried that tuxedo around for years, and when I left the band in St. Paul, I gave him back the trumpet." Nichols, with Beigel, played the Hotel Lowry, then headed east, but Beigel again stayed in the Twin Cities as Prohibition came to an end: "We left Kansas City, and then beer came back. We watched the beer trucks come in that night. We played there on the way to Minneapolis. We stopped in Omaha, Sioux City, and Sioux Falls for one-nighters and went on to the Lowry in St. Paul. We worked there for three weeks."

Beigel played the Leamington Hotel with Jack Malerich's band after leaving Nichols. Malerich was a piano player and an alumnus of the Minnesota Theater Band, a small orchestra of about thirty musicians who played in the 1920s. It was led by Lou Breese (Calabrese), who was preceded by Johnny Green, the composer of "Body and Soul."

Beigel compared the Twin Cities with the Chicago music scene in the era. "It was a melting pot mostly of the Nordic people," he said, "and then it got other people. We used to play a lot of schottisches and polkas in those days. But... they are still rhythmic." Beigel praised the Twin Cities' "beautiful symphony orchestra" and said that "music is a combination of pleasing sounds, and as long as you have melody, rhythm, harmony, tone and color, and you have form or style, what else is there?" Beigel also noted that in Minneapolis, as in Chicago, "Every Chinese restaurant had a band. The two Long brothers, Emmett and Dick, each ran a restaurant that featured music. One had the Golden Pheasant... [and the other] had a band across the street from the Leamington Hotel at the Curtis."

In 1924 violinist Dick Long had the band at the Nankin Cafe, and his brother Emmett played tenor sax with him along with Carl Bach on piano and Red Melby on banjo. Dick also had a three-piece band that played at Dayton's department store tearoom, while down a few floors in the basement of Hudson's Jewelers was a speakeasy known as Denny's. The Golden Pheasant was a walk-a-flight Chinese restaurant on Seventh Street across from the Radisson with a large sign out front and flashing colored lights. The food was good and the decor pleasant. Drummer Wally Anderson had the band there, featuring Don Cowan on sax, Norm Hendrickson on trombone, Art Swaline on piano, and Les Backer on guitar.

Recalling the period, Willie Hagen, who occasionally filled in on guitar, remembered "subbing for Doug Nash over at Murray's restaurant on Sixth Street across from the old Dyckman Hotel and at a wild nightclub over on Sixth called Curly's." He also helped his "banjo teacher Chester Gould at the Arcadia Ballroom, known as the Track, across from the courthouse on Fifth Street. We played continuous dime dances." In 1929 Hagen was lucky enough, with the help of Art Swaline, to join a band directed by Emory Granger in St. Paul. It played at "the beautiful Boulevards of Paris, a café on the corner of Lexington and University. It was probably the finest nightclub that ever hit the Twin Cities." During Prohibition "business just poured in. I had a signed contract with John Lane, the owner, who also owned the Coliseum [ballroom]. He had a lot of crazy gimmicks. Apparently he knew what a metronome was, for he would dash up and tell the bandleader, 'Try 99 instead of 94, the tempo is a bit too fast.' He was also credited with telling a bandleader to pick up the tempo because the music was slowing down by the time it got to the end of the hall. We started August '29 and ran through March 1930. I was paid $69 a week, which was pretty good money back then. The band would get through at one o'clock, and then Art Swaline would play a tiny piano out in the middle of the dance floor."

In the 1920s Norvy Mulligan's band played the Nicollet Hotel at Washington and Hennepin avenues, broadcasting on WLAG from noon to one. The Nicollet gig lasted for two years while Mulligan got the band into the Minneapolis Athletic Club for dinner music and the Miller Cafeteria on Seventh Street. When the Mulligan band returned to the Flame Room, singers Harry Cool and Kitty Willigan were out front. Mulligan played a style Roy Robison likened to that of Fats Waller: "He played [the same kind of] left-hand kind of tenths with his thumb. He would play a counter melody. It would never be the note of the melody. He wanted it to be kind

Norvy Mulligan's band held forth at the Radisson's Flame Room in Minneapolis, among other well-known nightspots. This 1939 group included, left to right, Doc Evans, Rollie Williams, Luke Leraan, Elmer Eberhardt, Dwight Hammond, Rollo Witham, and Mulligan.

of a counter melody. It was an individual style . . . Norvy was a fine singer of pop songs, too." Mulligan also had the band at the Nankin in 1928–29, featuring Doc Evans and Babe Eberhardt, guitarist Roland Williams, trombonist Luther Laraan, drummer Dwight Hammond, Rollo Witham, and Mulligan on piano.

Trombonist Hal Runyon, who would later play with Doc Evans, remembers the era as one when traveling and local groups often crossed paths at major venues. Runyon, born in Iowa in 1903, got his musical start in the air service after World War I. He played the fair circuit, gigged in Milwaukee, and ended up with the Ringling Brothers, Barnum and Bailey Circus band in Florida. When that got old, he responded to an ad in *Billboard* and landed a job with Little Benny's eleven-piece group, well known in Minnesota and Wisconsin. "One thing led to another, and I got a chance to join a band that was going to Minneapolis," said Runyon. "It was in the summertime. The band—the George Smith Steamboat Band—was only five or six pieces. They got their name from having been on a trip to China or Japan or someplace. Then they happened to get this good job booked in the Marigold for six months." The Marigold had a policy of booking two bands so it would have continuous music. The Guy Lombardo eight-piece band came into town expecting to dominate the scene. "Each member of the band had his own car and his own wife or companion riding with him—about eight cars for an eight-piece band," said Runyon. "They were Cadillacs, because they not only played good, but they wanted to look good. They had thought they would just bowl the people over at the Marigold, but the people liked us. We'd been there, and we got as much applause as Guy Lombardo did, which kind of surprised them. Took them down a notch."

Twin Cities–area music venues were not all so glamorous. Runyon noted a place near Anoka called the Old Mill. The man who owned it "also owned the Stables. They actually had been stables which had been used until recently for the fire department's horses. This man thought it would be a good place to open a nightclub, so he cleaned the place up, and we played there."

Runyon performed with several different bands at the Marigold, including Red Clark's, Oscar Westlund's and Harry Conners's. It was with Connors's band that he met early vibraphonist Red Norvo (Kenneth Norvill), later known as "Mr. Swing." Runyon said that Red "didn't play all night with the band. No, he'd just come up, and he'd do a special act. We'd play behind him. It was really just to get him acquainted with performing in front of people. He was good." Runyon said Norvo had a kind of slapping style with hard leather mallets: "It would just kind of 'plink.' It wouldn't ring afterwards." Runyon added that Norvo, who also played piano, was playing what he described as *real* jazz. Jazz was evolving a new language and moving beyond Dixieland music into new territory.

3

The Near Northside

"This has got to change. We've got to clean up this town."
—Hubert H. Humphrey, *mayor of Minneapolis, 1945*

During the last years of Prohibition and after its repeal in 1933, much of the best new jazz music could be heard in clubs and bars on Minneapolis's Near Northside and at the Cotton Club in suburban St. Louis Park. University campus jazz fans continued to enjoy the Dixieland sound, while other listeners sought out envelope-pushing players like trumpeter Rook Ganz and tenor sax great Lester Young at clubs and after-hours venues with more integrated audiences.

Minneapolis's bustling Near Northside neighborhood just outside downtown was home to most of the city's African Americans and its recent immigrant groups. Bars, restaurants, and clubs had prospered by offering a mix of illegal booze, jazz music, and late-night hours. Arthur Morton remembered jamming on the Near Northside as early as 1926: "Afro-American guys played so wonderful up there... including a trumpet player named Rook Ganz, who was absolutely a superb player. Everybody was drinking spiked beer."

When Minneapolis activist W. Harry Davis described the neighborhood for interviewers Dave Sletten and Kent Hazen, he included the infamous Howard's Steak House, known for both its music and after-hours activities. Howard's was a half block off Lyndale Avenue North. On one side was a drug store, Sam Shoar's Dry Goods, and Thelman's Grocery; on the other was Sam Bass Dry Goods and a Chinese laundry that later became a barber shop. Nearby was a drug store at Aldrich and Sixth next to Barney's Café, a pool hall, and the Nest, a music club, at Lyndale Place. Also close by were Landry's meat market, Emerson Lehman's Bakery (which became the Lincoln Delicatessen), and the Northside Bakery (which became the Brothers). It was a mixture of many colors and nationalities, black, Jewish, Irish.

Certain Northside residents lived outside the law. Ben Wilson, called the "Mayor of North Minneapolis," was arrested in a 1932 raid that seized moonshine whiskey at an establishment owned by Paul Turner. Turner was described in a Minneapolis newspaper as a "Negro musician and law student [who] opened a musicians club in North Minneapolis last week." Wilson, who operated several clubs on the Near Northside, had been involved in a shooting in 1925, although the prosecution failed to prove ownership of the confiscated liquor. After repeal, Wilson picked up fines for selling beer after 2 AM and for having two gambling devices in his Apex Club. On January 15, 1942, a newspaper noted that "a Negro and white mob scene was in progress on the third floor of the Clef Club at 637 Olson Blvd" at 3 AM when eighty-nine patrons "were arrested and carted off to the city jail." Among them was Wilson, the "mayor of Sixth Ave. N." Inside the Clef Club, police found "a juke box in operation, augmented by a five-piece orchestra." Three years later, Wilson and the popular, respected musician Rook Ganz were arrested together. Ganz, who had run afoul of the law more than once, was charged simply with "being found in a tippling house."

When Twin Cities old-timers recall their first exposure to jazz and the after-hours life, Rook Ganz's name invariably arises. Apart from his association with Wilson, Ganz was at home at some more respectable clubs, including the popular Cotton Club at 5916 Excelsior Boulevard in suburban St. Louis Park—not to be confused with the Near Northside's Cotton Club at Sixth Avenue North and Lyndale. The suburban club earlier bore the name El Patio ("PAY-show") and briefly reverted to that name but, like many clubs around the United States, it tried to cash in on the fame and notoriety of "the" Cotton Club in New York City, where Duke Ellington's band and others held sway. Many remembered the Twin Cities' Cotton Club as a speakeasy. After the repeal of Prohibition, co-owner Pete Karalis brought in Boyd Atkins to front the band. Karalis remembered that Ganz blew "a great, sweet, open horn . . . and used the megaphone as an extension to get a trombone affect on 'Solitude' and 'Sophisticated Lady.'"

One of the earliest assemblages of world-class talent on a Twin Cities stage was at the Cotton Club or El Patio in St. Louis Park. The 1934 band featured, left to right, Harold "Popeye" Booker, Adolphus Alsbrook, Walter Rouse, Bill Pugh, Boyd Atkins, Rook Ganz, and Lester Young.

Bands that played the Cotton Club in the thirties and forties can only be described as "all-star." Frankie Roberts said, "Boyd Atkins from Chicago was leader of the band. Lester Young played at El Patio. Lester had that cool sound on his horn more than Coleman Hawkins or Ben Webster. Not as much vibrato as most players then. I talked with Lester now and then, and sat in with him once in a while. It was Frankie Hines, Adolphus Alsbrook, Rook Ganz, Popeye Booker."

Early on in his tenure, which lasted until 1940, Atkins brought in Lester Young to replace Harry Pettiford on tenor sax. Harry's brothers, Oscar and Ira Pettiford, were in the black band that played for an exclusively white clientele. The band included Walter Rouse on guitar and drummer Bill Pugh. Looking back, Frankie Roberts concluded that the music scene in the Twin Cities in these years compared favorably with other parts of the country: "It was good. Guys would go out and people would get a chance to hear them play. You betcha."

El Patio may have gone by the name Pete's Place briefly in the mid-forties but eventually gave way to Culbertson's Café in 1947. Most recently, it housed Bunny's, which had moved from its original location a few blocks east on Excelsior Boulevard.

While the university campus's bands of the late 1920s and early 1930s were enthralled with Red Nichols and company, the ears of Twin Cities black musicians were focusing on more cutting-edge jazz developments presaging the coming Swing Era. These new sounds were already percolating among black musicians in places such as Kansas City, Chicago, and New York, and the music began to make its way into the local scene. The influential presence of Rook Ganz and Lester Young suggests the well-established circuit of black musicians shuttling between Kansas City, the Twin Cities, Chicago, New York City, and points between. Twin Cities listeners in the know enjoyed the privilege of hearing Lester Young's unique tenor saxophone style in full flower in their own backyard just before he burst onto the national scene to become a major influence on generations of musicians around the world.

Although *National Geographic* called St. Paul "a nine o'clock town," the highly regarded Rook Ganz—born Hilliard Thompson in 1904—played trumpet at Swing City on St. Paul's north side in the 1930s. Over the years Ganz rubbed elbows with many of the Twin Cities' musical elite—from the Pettiford family to Lester Young to symphony maestro Dmitri Mitropoulos.

In 1979, shortly before his death, Ganz recorded Clarence Williams's "Speakeasy Blues" with Ted Unseth's Americana Classic Jazz Orchestra. Unseth remarked that "Rook had the talent to make it big, but it would have meant being on the road much of the time, and he didn't want to leave his family, so he remained a local player all his life." In fact, when music bookings were slow, Ganz worked on road crews building highways and the cities' airport concourse. He still played weekends, though. "That's what you call enjoying your own habit," he said.

Many musicians remember Rook Ganz's skills. Legendary trumpeter Jabbo Smith, who in the 1920s was signed with Brunswick Records to compete with the sensational and popular sides being recorded by Louis Armstrong for the Okeh label, reminisced fondly about Rook Ganz and praised his skills as a jazz improviser. (Jabbo, Unseth, and the Wolverines played an extended engagement at the Commodore Hotel in St. Paul in 1976.)

Ganz, unlike many black musicians of his day, was not excluded from the Twin Cities' musicians' union, the American Federation of Musicians, and he served as secretary of Local 73 in 1936–37. The union's president at the time was Rook's cousin, who came up from Kansas City, Rook's hometown. Union member C. K. Running recalled that the union held jam sessions in the Musicians Club (part of today's Riverplace) and that the cousin came to town "during the Roosevelt vs. Landon election campaign wearing a giant sunflower. He was an engaging guy who made quite a contribution to what success the club had."

After first arriving in town from Winnipeg in 1931, Rook Ganz played at night spots including the Flame in downtown St. Paul and the Boulevard at Tenth and Olson Highway. Living on the Near Northside for a time, he became a regular at after-hours spots, where he jammed with the likes of trumpeter Roy Eldridge. Tommy Bauer remembered Ganz from the Northside clubs, as well as from the Club Deliza in south Minneapolis. Rook and Popeye Booker "would have Schlitz beer, made in St. Paul, with booze in it, and pass it around. Each of us would have a little taste."

Bassist Dave Faison recalled the 1930s when, as a high-school student, he played with Ganz: "I happened to know Rook. He asked me if I wanted to make some jobs with him." The twosome "played little Minnesota towns and Hap's Night Club out [Highway] 169 before Shakopee . . . Rook had a Model A Ford, and we'd [return] at six or seven in the morning, and I'd jump in and go to school." The jam sessions were also known for being competitive "cutting sessions," according to Jerry Mullaney: "If another player came in with a road band and we knew where he was going to be, just like Kansas City, we'd try to cut the guy. Sometimes we did. It was highly competitive and good fun."

Kent Hazen relates another Ganz tale based on Dixieland drummer Red Maddock's story about walking past Minneapolis's Ritz Hotel in 1932. Teenager Maddock heard music coming from the Spanish Village room, so he sat outside on the curb, listening, he said, to the greatest jazz he'd heard. When a man came out for a smoke, Red asked, "Are you in the band? I'd love to sing with the band or play drums with the band." He weighed about a hundred-and-ten wringing wet.

The player replied, "Yeah, my name is Rook Ganz." After Red told Ganz that he sang and danced, Ganz invited him to sit in and said, "Hide 'til we're sure there are no police." Red said that they played together, and people started throwing money because they liked the act. When Red got home his mother asked, "You haven't been stealing, have you?" Red replied, "No, people threw it." The next day his mother had his shoes shined and his pants pressed and said, "Go get 'em."

Ganz figured in a telling anecdote from a 1940s jam session in one of the Near Northside's after-hours joints. Visiting trumpeter Roy Eldridge dropped by late one night to join in. Since the band was already wailing, he sat down to unpack his trumpet. Meanwhile, Rook tore into the tune, working his magic in the middle range (he was not a high-note man). When Ganz finished, another prominent local trumpet man, Ira Pettiford, a high-note man, started to do the same thing a step up from Rook's range. At this point an amazed Eldridge began packing his horn back up. When asked what was wrong, he replied, "No sense in me bein' here!"

Although Ganz eventually gave up trying to make his living as a musician, he remains one of the Twin Cities' best-remembered players as well as a popular contributor at after-hours clubs. He was a regular at weekly jam sessions at Bucky's in Roseville as late as the 1970s, and he played at the original Artists' Quarter before his death in 1979. Maddock reminisced, "He'd get up with his table, chair, drink, and ash tray, and sit there on stage and look elegant—like he was a customer." As the memory of Prohibition faded and jazz became the popular music of the day with swing bands, after-hours activity slowed. But an element that the tolerant Twin Cities had seemingly avoided—racism—emerged as a more prevalent factor as the African American community became a bigger part of the local scene.

4

Prejudice in a Progressive Setting

"If a guy's got it, let him give it. I'm selling music, not prejudice."
—Benny Goodman

In the early years of jazz, the Twin Cities offered social and music scenes as integrated as those that existed in any American city. Minneapolis's and St. Paul's small African American populations in 1910—2,592 and 3,144, respectively—formed less than one percent of the state's total. By 1930, the percentage of blacks remained about the same (Minneapolis increasing to 4,176 and St. Paul to 3,981). Blacks began gravitating to Minneapolis for the same reasons that European immigrants did: jobs and economic opportunity. Positions as porters, waiters, and cooks were relatively plentiful, and hotels, notably the Metropolitan and the Ryan, were the largest employers of blacks. Large ballrooms provided some jobs for musicians, beginning in 1919 when Minneapolis's Marigold Gardens opened at Nicollet and Grant. Despite the Twin Cities' reputation for open-mindedness, those establishments remained lily white.

Musician Tela Burt, who arrived in Minneapolis in 1912, said that before World War I, "You'd go a week downtown, and if you saw three black people, you'd come back and say, 'My God, I saw three colored people.'" Burt started working at the Unique Theatre on Sixth and Hennepin: "This was vaudeville. Charlie Chaplin came while I was there. I used to run errands for him and all the old-timers. They had a bunch of white girls that did the dusting and cleaning the place after the show, you know, and I did the front. So, I got to run with them. They were inviting me over to their homes and forgot I was colored. The only time I knew I was colored was when I looked in the mirror . . . that's how I came to like Minneapolis."

Burt said some Twin Cities music clubs were integrated because the predominantly Scandinavian population at the time "didn't even know how to be prejudiced. The prejudice grew as the black population grew." He said that the Black Elks club put on what was known as the Manassas Ball with only black men and white women in attendance.

Jazz pianist and storyteller Nettie Hayes Sherman, who had trained at Boston Conservatory, entertained in the early 1920s at Than's, the St. Paul speakeasy and barbecue joint on Third Street (later Kellogg Boulevard) before it moved to a third-floor location on Jackson Street. She made seven dollars a week and "a lot of money in tips" from the clientele, which included politicians and gangsters. Her music, wrote Judy Henderson in a survey of African American music in Minnesota, was a blend of ragtime, Dixieland jazz, and popular tunes. Henderson said that much of Minnesota's early jazz was played by white musicians imitating the sounds of famous artists who toured the state, including at a later date players such as Count Basie, Duke Ellington, and Lionel Hampton: "Black players seldom played for white audiences, but white players joined their counterparts at some clubs, including Minneapolis's Clef Club, for late-night jam sessions."

Chicago native James Samuel Harris II, known as "Cornbread," came to Minneapolis as a youngster, took up the piano, and played every conceivable style and venue. Unlike Burt, he recalled facing considerable prejudice in the city: "Oh, you go in those ballrooms, and they'd look at you like, 'What in the world is this? Where did you come from? Hey Mister, that stuff on the floor needs sweeping up.' [I'd say] 'Wait a minute, I'm not here to sweep the floor. I'm here to dance.' 'Well, who you going to dance with? No, no, no, you ain't dancing with one of these white ladies. Hey, hit the door.'"

Longtime Minneapolis activist and newspaper editor Harry Davis, born in 1923, noted that Near Northside and St. Paul clubs in the Rondo and Dale neighborhood were hubs of musical activity and that black and white musicians had a unique relationship: "Regardless of what a musician thinks racially of another musician, there's always an appreciation if they're an artist. They like to learn from them ... Music did more for integration and human relationships than anything."

From his long perspective Davis said that Minneapolis was comparatively progressive, but racial segregation was the norm in the United States. When integration and desegregation began in the 1960s, black families sometimes experienced "frightening persecution in Minneapolis by individuals and groups behaving like the latter-day Ku Klux Klan in southern cities. These forces were still present in the city in 1971," said Davis, when he received the Democratic-Farmer-Labor party's endorsement as the city's first African American mayoral candidate supported by a major political party.

Prejudice also existed in the "enlightened" world at the University of Minnesota. Ken Green played boogie-woogie piano frequently in mixed-race groups there, often with his friend, bassist Oscar Pettiford. Green recalled, "We got him a forged fee statement for the university. He loved having it. He'd say, 'I'm going to the University of Minnesota' ... Oscar definitely liked the idea that we were white guys having something to do with him, and he had something to do with us. He was fiercely, fiercely conscious of racial injustice and striving for fair treatment."

Roy Robison, who knew the Twin Cities' jazz scene as far back as 1920, recalled that Oscar Pettiford's large and very talented musical family experienced racial prejudice and "never played on campus. Never did." There were, however, "good black bands around. I remember a black band that played regularly not too far from campus. They played at least Friday, Saturday, and Sunday nights ... Eli Rice and the Cotton Pickers, a fairly organized dance band."

Black bassist Dave Faison also said that players faced tough racial barriers: "In the thirties, you couldn't go in any of the clubs downtown. There were no mixed bands." Later, things hadn't improved much. In the forties he "went in to play at Augie's with Howard Brown's Band, and when we'd come off the stand, people would want to mix with the band, but Augie would send us downstairs. It was a thing that always stuck with me." He continued that Augie "wouldn't give us drinks ... so Brown said, 'I'll fix him.' Each guy would take a turn bringing in a case of beer each night. Then we'd leave the bottles on the table and next day they'd all be cleaned off. It was Howard's turn, and as he came out of the cooler,

Augie comes down and said, 'So that's why all those bottles have been here.'" According to Faison, Augie was so ashamed that the next night "when we came to work, he had a booth up in front where we could sit and mingle. People would buy the band drinks, which was very profitable for him."

One of the Twin Cities' best-known and -loved musicians, saxophonist Irv Williams, arrived in the Twin Cities during World War II as part of an all-black band at Wold Chamberlin Naval Air Station. He settled in—reluctantly at first, comparing the Twin Cities' artistic and racial scene negatively with St. Louis: "It was terrible, just awful. Number one, you go down Hennepin Avenue, and there wasn't a black face anywhere. Just on Sixth Avenue North. The club El Patio in St. Louis Park had a black band. St. Paul at the foot of Rice Street had very few black musicians." He continued, "Why? I can't blame it on prejudice. There just weren't enough guys around. When I organized the navy band, they had to take notice, but there *was* prejudice then. I went to Augie Ratner, who had a joint on Fifth and Hennepin. I went down and did an audition, and he liked the band, but he told me, 'I gotta hire either black or white.' I said, 'Hire black,' so he says, 'I don't think so, right now.'"

Irv Williams tried to confront discrimination against black musicians but said he had little success with B'Nai B'rith and the Urban League. Then the president of the Minneapolis musicians' union, George Murk, "went up and down Hennepin Avenue, so they tell me, and the club owners said, 'No, we don't want any black musicians.' I went to Stanley Ballard, secretary of the union. Then I *really* didn't get any work. I got back here in 1944–45, a whole year without work, so I got a job in the dry cleaning industry."

Williams broke back into music at the new Calhoun Beach Club after the war. In the club's ballroom, Bob Dean played lead alto, Stu Anderson played bass, and Bill West played trumpet. "We had four saxes, trumpet, and three rhythm. That's how I broke in and started getting jobs. The union never really said anything other than that I was out of my head. I just kept my mouth shut and I started working. There was a lady at the union who was very insulting. Ira Pettiford and a couple of others were the only black guys in the union," Williams recalled, "but in St. Paul, they had Rook Ganz, Adolphus Alsbrook, Frank Hines. It was de facto segregation . . .

Black musicians were working. St. Paul was a jumpin' town at that time because of the leaders of that union."

Although singer Dick Mayes met with relative success and acceptance on the Twin Cities' music scene, he described the cities' racial situation as "terrible, absolutely terrible" and downtown Minneapolis as "notorious... You never saw black bands down there—Harry's, Charlie's, Freddy's." Mayes, who called himself a rebel, remembered working at the Flame on Nicollet Avenue with Percy Hughes: "Ray Perkins and the Franski brothers told Percy, 'Don't have black players out front on the break.' I said, 'F___ you,' and went around and talked to everyone. The union wasn't any better. They had jobs to give away, but black musicians never got the free jobs."

But Mayes said there was another side to the racial coin: "One of the reasons I liked the business so much was that ninety percent didn't care [about color]. They'd help you, but not so with owners and booking agents." Mayes had a pair of highly successful engagements in the 1960s at the top of the Sheraton Ritz in the Golliwog Lounge. Bobby Peterson and Manfredo Fest were the pianists on separate bookings. Dave King played drums, and Jay Goetting was on bass. But work again became sparse: "We went for about a year after playing the Golliwog. I got angry. We held a record for attendance. No one had as many people as we did until John Denver" came along in 1969.

Most jazz players would probably concur that musicians usually had less racial prejudice simply because they respected each other's playing. Even clubs that specialized in performing Dixieland with mostly white players mixed it up. Drummer Bill Schneider said musicians were all on the same page musically: "Standard tunes are standard tunes. If they're played by Rook Ganz, they are played in one style. If they're played by Doc Evans, they are played in another style, but they still follow the basic structure of the tune. So you got along."

5

The Musicians' Unions

"Sometimes you need to stand with your nose to the window and have a good look at jazz. And I've done that on many occasions."

—J. J. Johnson

From the earliest years of jazz music, the Twin Cities musicians' union served an important function as gatekeeper to paying jobs. The union supported musicians' rights to reasonable wages and tried to enforce policies aimed at the owners of clubs and larger music venues. The American Federation of Musicians, chartered in 1897, helped many players secure the best-paying jobs available in the towns. Musician and researcher Carl Warmington said that for many years the musicians' union "effectively controlled employment."

Joining the American Federation of Musicians involved a performance test, said Warmington. The office and club rooms of the Minneapolis local were on Glenwood Avenue, "a convenient congregating place where one might pick up a playing date, shoot pool, play cards, and be served a light lunch. In addition there was a club bootlegger who vended moonshine in special-size bottles; the half pint was a comfortable pocket size and was supplied when you asked for an 'E-flat.'"

Musicians "needed a union card to play with the top bands on the university campus." Roy Robison said that in the early days "to become a member of the best campus bands, even then you had to be a member of the union. Even the kids had to. You couldn't get anywhere without being a union member. A good share of them couldn't read music, so it was kind of [a] put-on thing. They'd go down [to the union hall] and... they'd know what was going to be put up in front of them. They would play 'Dinah' or whatever it was by ear, and, yes, they would pass the test. I can think of campus musicians who couldn't read a note of music, really."

While neither Minneapolis nor St. Paul had separate unions for blacks and whites, many theaters, nightclubs, and even the symphony orchestra had de facto policies of segregation. The American Federation of Musicians itself did not officially allow blacks to join until the early forties, but Julie Ayer points out in *More Than Meets the Ear* that "the federation also ruled that if a black musician were denied admission to a local, he or she could join the nearest local that would accept the musician and should receive all the privileges of membership of that local."

The union, although racially restrictive, did not oppose the integrated jam sessions and after-hours activities which flourished in the 1920s and '30s in the Twin Cities. Dave Faison recalled, "The Twin Cities didn't have black and white unions. If you played outside your local, you had to get traveling money. You had to belong to two locals. If there was a ten-piece band and one guy was from Minneapolis, the whole band had to get travel pay." The pay scale for a three-hour performance during Prohibition was six dollars, pretty good money for those days. It went a long way toward tuition for campus musicians, or toward the twenty-five dollars it took to purchase a Model T Ford.

The musicians' union became not just a clearing house and gathering place but a way for players to hook up with each other. Drummer Kenny Horst first learned of fabled Twin Cities tenor man Irv Williams through Kenny's father, who worked at the union: "My dad used to tell me about this tenor player at Mauer's [later the Sherwood]."

For years the union was powerful and able to look out for its members (support that some members today fear has been lost). In the 1940s jazz announcer Leigh Kamman was working with Sid Smith doing a Saturday-afternoon record show called *The Swing Club*. Kamman said that jazz impresario and producer Norman Granz "came in, semi-arrogant, and made us an offer of a small percentage of the net proceeds if we'd promote the Jazz at the Philharmonic Concert at the Minneapolis Auditorium." Later on, at KSTP in the 1960s, Kamman "began to do live broadcasts from Freddy's, and if they were Norman Granz's artists, he'd make sure they were well paid and adhered to union agreements. He became warm and cordial and an absolutely ethical guy."

A number of well-known players served in official capacities in Local 30 in St. Paul and Local 73 in Minneapolis, when they were separate entities and since their merger in 1981. Rook Ganz was the secretary of Local 73 in the 1930s, an unusual position since most black musicians were not yet allowed in the union. Dixielander Doc Evans was a board member whose last worldly activity was a meeting at the Local 73 office in 1977.

One top bandleader from the 1920s and 1930s, Norvy Mulligan, had the experience of being tossed out of the union in 1938. Jimmy Robb remembered, "In those days the union was very strong, and you couldn't function without being a member... Tippling in the music business? If you were on the radio, probably not; if you were in the honky-tonks, OK." Mulligan sold insurance and remained outside the music scene until colleague Hal McIntyre started a big band. "We became reinstated amateurs," said Robb, and Norvy rejoined the union in 1975.

Trombonist Hal Runyon said there was a time in most young musicians' careers when becoming a union member was mandatory: "I got on the train and got to La Crosse. One of the boys in the band met me and said, 'Do you belong to the union?' I said, 'No.' He said, 'I'll get you up there, and we'll get you into the union right away, because you've got to be in the union in order to work here.' So I joined the union."

Bassist Adolphus Alsbrook said he and his colleagues in Rook Ganz's band were forced to leave the union when Pete Karalis hired them from the soon-to-be-defunct Apex Club to work at the Cotton Club in 1934: "They thought they'd take a chance, and they hired us. But they wouldn't hire us through the union, so everybody gave up his union card to take the job. We got in a little trouble 'cause we were non-union, but [Karalis and] the Greeks didn't want to be controlled by the union. They were four fine guys plus Pete and his dad. In fact, he got us out of jail one night. [We were] jammin' about one o'clock and the police backed up and took a hundred-and-some people out of the place. Pete's dad come down there and bail us all outta jail."

Union secretary Stanley Ballard said that December '41 had been the best ever in union jobbing history for local musicians. Writing in *Down-Beat,* Don Lang said Local 73's biggest New Year's Eve came in 1942. A few years later Twin Cities musicians made national headlines when staff musicians at KSTP struck the Radio City studios in Minneapolis. In July 1944, KSTP's boss, Stanley Hubbard, asked the chairman of the War Labor Board to request that President Franklin Roosevelt use wartime powers to take over the Minneapolis musicians' union and order the sixteen striking musicians back to work. A two-year accord was reached, based on a similar agreement with WCCO. Staff musicians would receive $52.50 a week for twenty-two hours plus two weeks' vacation.

In 1960 one of the union's most well-known performers, bassist Biddy Bastien, took on the important post as secretary-treasurer of Minneapolis's Local 73. Bastien's son David said his father "believed that music ought to be a professional craft governed by a strong union." David described his father's passionate involvement: "He was committed, against all odds, to keeping music as a viable profession." His father's strong beliefs "alienated many of the younger musicians, who believed that they should be allowed to work for substandard wages. He insisted . . . that no non-union musicians could work with his members and that no musicians should work for less than scale."

Former Twin Cities pianist and radio personality Herb Schoenbohm, who occasionally played tuba at Metropolitan Stadium, said Biddy Bastien could be a tough union representative. Biddy took on WCCO and Calvin Griffith, owner of the Minnesota Twins, for using the house organist at Metropolitan Stadium to play the national anthem, which was, by contract, supposed to be played at every game by a small brass band of union members. When Cal said he no longer would honor the contract, Biddy made one call to the Teamsters, who informed the Twins head office that they would not allow their drivers delivering beer to cross the picket lines, "and without beer, you know the rest of the story!"

Since union rules prevented the secretary-treasurer from playing professionally, Biddy could not perform. He worked instead to develop strong alliances with other labor officials and political figures. He also labored tirelessly to integrate the national union, which still had some segregated locals in 1960 when he took office, and he was actively involved in the civil rights movement in the Twin Cities. In 1968 Biddy returned to his "true profession—playing." Biddy acknowledged, "It was a hard, thankless job, and I'm glad I did it. I don't think I'd ever do it again."

Across the river, Dick Kadrie, a longtime member of the Pappy Trester Band at the Park Nite Club on Snelling in St. Paul, was elected president of St. Paul Local 30 in 1951. In the early eighties, he served on the board of directors of Local 30–73 after their merger. He played at the Magic Bar in Minneapolis and with many road bands in the thirties and forties.

With all but a handful of working musicians belonging to the union for years, many players have tales—mostly positive—about their experiences in the labor organization. Drummer Joe Kimball, who played with Jerry Dibble's band as well as numerous clubs around the Twin Cities and beyond, recalled, "My first job after the war ended was at Schooner's Tavern in South Minneapolis with John Robertson's band. The group played until the 20 percent cabaret tax was put into effect. The group was fired, but because they had a contract, the union sued and got them their money."

Not all comments about the union are positive. In 1994, Ken Green, a founder of the Twin Cities Jazz Society, noted that obstinate club owners helped stoke the fires of player discontent. Owners, he said, "still don't want to pay the guys . . . but the guys . . . are what you'd call 'willing victims.' They've all gotten out of the union. The union never did anything. The reward as I see it now is that they are playing for about thirty-to-thirty-five dollars a night."

Cornetist Doc Evans underscored the fact that not everyone held the union in high esteem: "I was a sideman in one of the best and most conscientious local bands I ever played with. We were working a Hennepin Avenue club owned by an ex-bootlegger. One night, at the end of the week, we were told we were through as of that night. When the leader remarked that the union rules required two weeks' notice, we were told if any member went to the union 'the boys' would take care of us. I'm afraid we didn't quite have the courage of our convictions, and the band broke up then and there."

Conditions for players today are not good. Local president Brad Eggen, a crusader for better wages for jazz musicians and fair treatment by employers, lamented in the Twin Cities Jazz Society newsletter, "Your home town treats jazz musicians like second-class wage earners. The system of compensating the jazz musician frequently lacks honor and integrity. When every other financial commitment on a jazz engagement has been fulfilled, the musicians still get stiffed." Last minute cancellations, eleventh-hour demands for early setup and extra time, and unexpected deductions from paychecks plague local players. Twin Cities resident and internationally

Busy vocalist Debbie Duncan still finds time to volunteer at the Youth Jazz Camp, which is avidly supported by the musicians' union.

known jazz organist Jack McDuff said in a 1994 interview, "I've seen gigs around here where guys get twenty or twenty-five dollars a night." The love of music and the need to play dominate, he noted: "If we were all millionaires, most of us would still play."

Unfortunately, many players no longer get formal contracts, nor do they pay dues to the union. This reduces union revenue that could be used to enforce wage and benefit agreements. Former Twin Cities Jazz Society president Jerry Swanberg says that most jazz musicians today are not union members. Local 30–73 had some 3,000 members when the Minneapolis and St. Paul chapters merged. In 2010, there were around

1,360, according to Tom Baskerville: "We still have a majority of the musicians who make their living primarily by performing music. Whether that is a majority, I just don't know. There's a lot of musicians out there."

According to Brad Eggen, the high-profile jazz musicians in the community, "those who earn a significant wage and have a strong professional reputation, are nearly all in the American Federation of Musicians (AFM). Many also perform AFM musical theater shows, do AFM jingle recordings, or work with established large AFM ensembles. Many work union trust-fund engagements." He notes that "the pension program is significant, and the recently established medical voucher plan can help anyone unable to get insurance from other sources. Twin Cities Jazz Society concerts pay union pension contributions."

Today, the musicians' union recognizes that music is a bit like organized baseball, with young players coming up forming a farm system of sorts. To engage young musicians, Bernie Edstrom and others started the Youth Jazz Camp in 2001. More than 170 students are being served annually. Baskerville emphasized, "This is not an 'all-star jazz camp.' Students of virtually all levels are accepted." The union has been solidly behind the educational effort, and musicians like Eric Gravatt, Dean Brewington, and Debbie Duncan volunteer their time. Perhaps there is a stronger future for the union ahead, although it seems to be the symphony orchestras that are keeping the union coffers at least partially filled. Union participation by jazz and pop musicians continues to wane.

6
On the Avenue

Nightly, lights are shining brightly,
Feet are tripping lightly
While the music plays.
Madness in the guise of gladness,
Overcoming sadness
In a million ways.

—"Boulevard of Broken Dreams,"
HARRY WARREN and AL DUBIN

New York has its Great White Way. San Francisco has Broadway and Chicago its Miracle Mile. Minneapolis has its seven-mile-long Hennepin Avenue, known simply as "the Avenue" by the musicians who played on a short downtown stretch from Washington Avenue to Ninth Street.

Virtually all of the musicians associated with jazz in the Twin Cities in the fifties, sixties, and seventies played the Avenue, most in "stage bars," a euphemism for strip joints. But Hennepin has also been home to theaters that once hosted the country's top musical names who passed through on the Orpheum circuit or played other popular venues beginning in the 1920s.

Among the earliest known memories of jazz and live music on the Avenue are Tela Burt's recorded recollections of the Unique Theater, where he ran errands for Charlie Chaplin when vaudeville was the primary, if waning, brand of entertainment. Programs often went on for hours, and music was an important part of the mix. Pianist Eubie Blake was frequently in the shows. An entertainment headline in the June 21, 1925, *Minneapolis Journal* heralded, "Jazz Week Program at Hennepin Brings Back Isham Jones." Jones's band played a prominent role in an otherwise mostly comedic review at the Hennepin-Orpheum that included Jane Green "among the leaders of the jazz vocalists."

Paul Whiteman, whose band blended highly orchestrated, danceable jazz with classical and pop, played the Minnesota Theater on Hennepin in 1928, when he was interviewed for the *Minneapolis Sunday Tribune.* The "King of Jazz" called his brand of entertainment "essentially an American product." He said he didn't understand why someone of means hadn't financed a series of jazz concerts: "Jazz is educational, you know. And it has raised the musical appreciation of the country to an unprecedented degree." He continued, "The other day I stepped into a taxicab and heard the driver whistling one of the more intricate passages from *Rhapsody in Blue.* I asked him what he was whistling, and he told me as though it was the most ordinary thing in the world. Jazz has educated people." Refuting the idea that jazz had at least some of its roots in Africa, Whiteman said, "That's all rot . . . It is purely American music, and like America, has something of every other location in it."

Twin Cities Dixieland legend Doc Evans remembers attending Whiteman's 1928 concert at the Minnesota Theater. He recalled enthusiastically, "They had Bix, the Rhythm Boys with Bing Crosby—almost anyone you can name. I took a sack of sandwiches along and stayed all day. Spent the time between stage shows out in the lobby."

Writer Les Saefke said Whiteman always opened with Gershwin's *Rhapsody in Blue:* "It signaled the start of great Whiteman tunes, which seemed to always center on little Mike Pingatore setting the pace with the lively strumming of his banjo. Whiteman had a subtle sense of humor and would especially delight the ladies in the wiggling of his huge frame to the varied tempo of 'Well Diggers Hoedown.' He was a startling sight striding through the foyer in his all-white Panama hat and suit, chauffeured around town in an all-white coupe."

Along "the Avenue" near the Minnesota Theater was the Palace Theater at 424 Hennepin, a few doors down from the Paradise, an after-hours spot in the 1930s. A block up at 520 Hennepin was the Camel's Club, also a late-night hangout, which closed in 1936. Farther up Hennepin, near Eighth Street, was an upstairs speakeasy called Galleries. Pianist Art Goldberg (Arthur Morton), considered one of the best at the time, played there in 1930 before moving to Hollywood, where he composed movie and television scores.

Almost every musician who played professionally in the decades before and after World War II has a story that somehow relates to the Avenue. Twin Cities pianist Jim Trost started playing resorts like Yellowstone and Mammoth Lakes around age twenty, an experience that exposed him "to another level of jazz and acquainted me with some older, very competent jazz musicians with whom I played as often as possible." He continued casual jobbing while in college and then "took an interesting job during the summer of 1958 playing at the Saddle Bar in Minneapolis, a dive on lower Hennepin Avenue where, beginning at nine o'clock every night, three female strippers an hour would remove most of their clothes to music for the edification of an all-male audience." Their routine, he said, "was simple and invariable: one slow tune followed by a medium-tempo song and finally one fast-tempo number to close each dancer's set. Since the strippers had little appreciation or concern for the music, we played 'straight ahead' jazz while the drummer would catch an occasional bump or grind with a rim shot or drum roll."

According to Trost, the musicians "were excellent partly because this was one of the highest-paying steady jobs in Minneapolis at the time. However, many were addicted to heroin, which sometimes caused them to nod out on the last set. The 'girls,' on the other hand, kept performing regardless of the fading background, and I hammered away to help compensate for the diminishing number of notes and volume from the saxophone." Trost recalled accompanying "the dancing of such virtuosos as Miss Dairy Queen (also known as Miss Milky Way), named for breasts of a size that seemed to defy human variation; Lola DeTour, a veteran of many campaigns and somewhat beyond age forty; and Athena, the Grecian Goddess, an attractive young lesbian from rural Georgia, as well as a myriad of others." Trost remembered that "contrary to the expectations of my friends who came to hear me, I very quickly lost interest in naked female bodies in these circumstances. I focused on the music, which, at times, really got to cooking. Our band was musically compatible and worked well together."

The scene was a 1947 Christmas party at the Glenwood Chalet featuring Bill West on trumpet; Eric Giere, sax; Jeanne Peterson, piano; Ray Palmer, bass; Bob Pope, drums; and an unknown vocalist.

In the early days, Hennepin Avenue East hosted two labor temples and a union hall, all of which featured live music and the jazz of the day on a regular basis. Saxophonist Percy Hughes would sneak in the back of the Labor Temple at Central and Hennepin to listen to the music. In 1939, he likely heard the great Jimmy Lunceford band. Near the temple was Robert's Cafe, where Eric Giere, Bob Caldwell on guitar, and Ray Johnson on bass later held forth. Johnson also played with drummer Bill Blakkestad and pianist Andy Bergen at Robert's.

While there are many stories of musicians who overindulged—Blakkestad tales are legend—many of the players were pretty straight. Drummer Russ Moore remembers, "Ray Johnson was older than the rest of us. When Chubby Jackson came out with the five-string bass, Ray stayed with four but used a high C. He wouldn't mingle, but went to the band room with a lunch bucket with sandwiches and coffee. Bob Pope would order a glass of water, put a fizzie in it, and have a peanut butter sandwich."

It was during Prohibition that the area around Washington and Hennepin avenues began to develop as an entertainment mecca. Several theaters already existed, both the State and the Orpheum having been built in 1921. The State has little musical history, but the Orpheum at Ninth and Hennepin played host to vaudevillians, swing bands, jazz artists, and shows. It was called a "junior" Orpheum after the larger, older original on Seventh Street. Even at that, the newer Orpheum was considered the largest vaudeville theater in the United States. It featured the bands of Benny Goodman, Tommy Dorsey, Count Basie, and others during the Swing Era. Writer Les Saefke recounted the bands that graced the Orpheum's stage, from "name" bands to the Minneapolis North High Swing Ensemble. Woody Herman's First Herd brought the house down with solos by Flip Phillips, Bill Harris, and then-local piano player Lou Levy. Cab Calloway was another jazz hit with saxophonists Charlie Parker and Chu Berry, bebop trumpeter Dizzy Gillespie, and singer Billy Eckstine. (Today's Orpheum, purchased in 1959 by theater mogul Ted Mann, is currently owned by the Hennepin Theatre Trust.)

Augie's—to this day a fixture on the Avenue—had a reputation for keeping jazz musicians employed, and also for being one of the real dives of lower Hennepin. It shares the same address, 424 Hennepin Avenue, as the once well-known Palace Theater. Augie's was known as Lindy's Café when it first opened in the 1930s, then became Crombie's, where Les Beigel once had a Dixieland band, and finally Augie's in 1944, with Howard Brown and the Rhythm Kings on stage.

Despite all the clubs, not many black musicians played on the Avenue. Twin Cities saxophone legend Irv Williams said that despite pressure from the musicians' union, club owners didn't want black musicians there. After World War II, when white GIs returned home looking for jobs and housing, many gains that African Americans had made were lost. Southern blacks who had moved north were crowded in segregated sections of the inner city, while whites discovered new places to live in the suburbs. In Minneapolis in the late 1940s, African Americans were the largest minority, but the school system had no black teachers. The Minneapolis

Urban League was still a small operation and unable to change practices and biases on the Avenue.

Many well-known Twin Cities musicians played nightspots on the Avenue over the years. Herman Mitch, who would become a prominent jazz entrepreneur, owned the Casablanca (later the Gay '90s), 408 Hennepin, which had a long bar in the back. A trio led by Jack Widener played up front. Babe Wagner had a short stint there with Gene Krupa but eventually left Minneapolis for his native New Ulm to lead an old-time band. Red Dougherty had a Dixie group at the Casablanca that included such luminaries as Doc Evans, Hal Runyon, Frankie Roberts, Biddy Bastien, and Eddie Tolck.

Augie Ratner, owner of Augie's, wasn't above stealing talent on the Avenue. Eddie Berger and his colleagues had been playing in Wisconsin when they were "discovered" about 1960 by Vic Levine and hired to play at his club: "Vic booked us up here for a couple of weeks at Fifth and Hennepin, and we did good there . . . We just played our own thing." When Augie Ratner saw the band, he contacted the group's booking agency in Chicago, and because Augie paid more money than Vic, "the second time we came back, we played Augie's." Vic's, at 507 Hennepin, which opened in 1951 and was previously known as the Dome, was where Harry Blons was crowned as "The King of Dixieland" and such notables as Henry "Red" Allen and pianist Joe Turner performed. (Vic's became Osterberg's in 1957.)

Something of a jazz war broke out in 1954 when Doc Evans had his group at Williams Bar at Sixth and Hennepin. Three of his players, Warren Thewis, Loren Helberg, and Bob Greunenfelder, jumped ship to join Tommy McGovern's "Original Minneapolis Jazz Band" at the Saddle. Evans reconstituted his group and said of his new competition, "They won't be as authentic. When they were with me, I always had to fight to keep them from playing swing, and now I think they're likely to get out of control." Evans's trombonist Hal Runyon entered the fracas, recalling that Nate Shapiro booked the Original Minneapolis Dixieland Band at Lindy's in 1937. Even then, McGovern had a rival band around the corner at Curly's, but the musicians frequently got together to jam.

While there was not much fraternization between players and strippers on the Avenue—although some recalled a few marriages—the Avenue was life changing for many musicians. The Brass Rail didn't have strippers,

Pianist Red Dougherty fronted this band at the Casablanca on Hennepin Avenue, Minneapolis, in 1943, including Hal Runyon on trombone, Biddy Bastien on bass, Doc Evans on cornet, Frankie Roberts, clarinet, and Eddie Tolck, drums. The club would later be known as the Gay '90s.

but it did have cheap drinks, so many players would head for the Rail on their breaks. Drummer Lee Pierson kicked addiction and found religion when a stripper talked him into playing less and going into the ministry at Galilee Lutheran Church in St. Paul. Father Bill McGrade, who was president of the Twin Cities Jazz Society, attended jam sessions sponsored by the society. He and Pierson would move to a corner and discuss deep theological matters while others played.

Pianist Jan Jacobson noted that Pierson was considered a great strip drummer: "Very smooth. These were jazz jobs, but the drummers had to catch the show." Gary Berg agreed, "The drummers were the only ones that had anything to do with the show." Pierson played McGuire's

Duffy's at Twenty-sixth and Twenty-sixth in Minneapolis boasted consistent quality music in the early 1950s. Performers Loren Helberg, Hal Runyon, Warren Thewis, Tommy McGovern, and Doc Evans.

in Arden Hills with guitarist Reuben Ristrom and tenor man Bob Crea. When Pierson was killed helping someone change a tire on the side of the road, Ristrom recalled that Bob Crea, "the best jazz tenor sax player we ever had, played at Lee's funeral service with me." Crea died less than a year later.

Eddie Berger concurred that most Hennepin strip-club musicians barely noticed the strip dancers for whom they played. Instead, he recalled, "One of the great sidelights of working Augie's was that Augie was a lightweight fighter, and Friday nights the Gillette fights were on TV. He'd set up a TV set on this little stage while the girls would be dancing. Augie was a funny dude. Pay was Monday night, which was also his gambling night. If he lost, he'd pound on the door; if he won, it was tap-tap-tap."

The teenage pianist Bobby Lyle, named almost universally as one of the finest musicians to have come out of the Twin Cities, also played at Augie's. Eddie Berger, who was at Augie's when Duke Page was thrown out, said he "hired Bobby for one of his first gigs when he was eighteen years old. He was playing great, man. Augie didn't want him in there because he was black and because he was underage. Augie wouldn't let him stay in on the breaks—he made him go to the hamburger joint across the street. I had Lyle in there for a couple of weekends. Augie could never understand that one."

Most players on the Avenue had jazz engagements besides the strip gigs; working seven nights was not unusual. Berger also played the Saddle and the Frolics, a club which opened in 1947 at 516 Hennepin and shifted down to Third Street ten years later as the New Frolics. Musicians frequently moved from club to club. Jan Jacobson recalled a gig with Bob Crea, who had let go a hot organist from Kansas City. Jan said Crea "would call a tune, and you'd say 'What key?' and Crea said, 'I don't know, just give me a note,' then you'd start looking for the key, and wonder, 'Where are we?' That was a lot of fun because you learned a lot—quick. The [Hammond] B-3 was just coming into its own, and the organ band was doing better than most jazz groups. It supplanted the piano because it had the bass notes." (The B-3 has both bass pedals and a section under the left hand that allows the operator to play an electronic "bass line.")

Ron Seaman played piano at Augie's with drummer Ray Olson's band in the early sixties and then again after a stint with the U.S. Army: "I'm always amazed at all the guys who say they played at Augie's. When I was gone from '64 to '66, Russ Peterson and Tom Slobodzian were there. I heard similar stories about young guys playing there underage and that we never played what the girls wanted, but there were summer nights when six or more clubs in a four-block radius had top-level jazz players working... all playing 'A Train'!" The bands rarely played what the strippers wanted anyway, and they thought it was great fun to play John Coltrane's "Giant Steps" when the girls expected "Kansas City."

Not everyone played the Avenue. Dave Karr noted, "Some guys enjoyed playing the strip bars. They could play anything they wanted; there was no bass, just drums, keyboard, and a horn. I didn't like those dives myself."

In the sixties on the Avenue, it was Augie's, the Saddle, Roaring Twenties, Copper Squirrel, Gay '90s, the Happy Hour, and some even sleazier

Bob Crea was a veteran not only of the Avenue but of groups as diverse as the Wolverines Classic Jazz Orchestra and the Buddy Rich Band. He swung hard—and lived hard and died too young, in 1980.

joints on the side streets. The dancers, to a girl, according to pianist Ron Seaman, wanted "Night Train," "Misty," "Satin Doll," and a few other standards. The musicians were first rate: Mickey McClain, Jerry Rusch, Don Milleon, Dick Bortolussi, Don Rustad, Jim Marentic, Kenny Horst, Dick LaVay, Bob Rockwell, and a host of others. "We never had a bass player," said Ron Seaman. "The piano was expected to play the bass lines. We would trot out three dancers per set and just blow jazz for each one as she wandered up and down a six-foot plank hovering over the mostly lonely guys below. The bandstand was a tiny space above the bar with barely enough room for three guys. I remember finding some New Year's Eve decorations up there from 1947, which would indicate how often that area was cleaned." Seaman also said it could get rough on the Avenue: "Kenny Horst was slugged on a break once, Norm Lien was held up at gunpoint on the way to his car, and a well-known Twin Cities musician suffered a breakdown on stage."

The Avenue was always a popular place for Twin Citians to go slumming. These "respectable" people marched as a group from strip club to strip club, laughing and drinking their way up and down Hennepin. This weekend activity "gave them great water-cooler fodder for Monday morning." (In recent times, Augie's has made an attempt to polish its image, at least in name. Twenty-first century listings for entertainment on Hennepin include Augie's Bourbon Street Cabaret and Augie's Theater Lounge in what is known as the Warehouse District in Minneapolis.)

Although the musicians' union exercised considerable power in the Twin Cities, it was severely put to the test when club owners decided to ditch live performances in favor of recorded music on tapes or in jukeboxes. At first, bassist Biddy Bastien, secretary of Minneapolis Local 73, had moderate success keeping live music on the Avenue. He understood the financial squeeze the club owners were feeling: "From a business standpoint (recorded music) would be sensible for them. I had to use all of my techniques to keep them from moving right in."

Finally, in January 1972, Hennepin Avenue musicians went on strike. One newspaper headline read, "Jukeboxes to replace bands?" Pianist Jan Jacobson, a regular player on the Avenue, identified the main cause of the strike as being the club owners' decision to "drop out of the on-sale liquor-dealers association so they didn't have to uphold the agreement

Reuben Ristrom has long been one of the most in-demand musicians in the Twin Cities and serves as a member of the musicians' union board of directors.

with the musicians' union. That forced us out on the street with twenty-below weather and twenty-five mile-an-hour winds down Hennepin. It put the whole avenue on notice that taped music was gonna take over the scene." Jacobson concluded, "That was the beginning of the end." The going scale around 1960 had been $108 a week, according to Jacobson, and it had soon bumped up to $135. "It was hard to become inventive," he said. "The live music made the show; after tapes, it fell apart. It killed the Avenue, but playing there made for much better musicians."

Guitarist and union board member Reuben Ristrom recalled that during the 1972 strike he picketed some clubs downtown although he was "working at a suburban motel lounge and not affected by the strike against the on-sale liquor dealers." Pianist Mickey McClain noted the owners had gotten tapes even prior to the threatened labor action, and although he feared it could lead to less work, he always felt the owners had the right to use recorded music. President Brad Eggen of combined union Local 30–73 says the standoff was much more complicated and significant: "There was litigation between the American Federation of Musicians and alleged employers in Chicago about that time which resulted in an agreement between the AFM and the National Labor Relations Board. It was decided that bar owners on casual engagements may not be and usually are not the employer, so bars do not have to negotiate with the AFM." This decision, said Eggen, "made a huge change in the industry. It eliminated one of the focal roles of the union and a major source of security in the music industry."

One face, one sound, one name that was ubiquitous on the Avenue for years was Eddie Berger. His impish countenance and his clear alto sax tone could be heard at Vic's and Augie's and, because he occasionally filled in for other players, at spots like the Saddle and off Hennepin at the Artists' Quarter or Lake Street's Padded Cell. Berger, a Philadelphia native, started playing a handmade recorder-like instrument as a kid, and his first listening experiences came in the early forties. "Benny Goodman was the first jazz musician I really got interested in," he said. Eddie liked growing up in Philly, although his parents weren't jazz aficionados: "My parents were very happy having beer parties and singing 'Sweet Adeline' with some cat who would come over and play piano . . . They'd always play in some strange key, you know, and they'd always play the right changes for these sing-alongs. It was wild, man."

Eddie soon began to reserve copies of the latest Charlie Parker 78s at the local record store. He and his friends would listen to them and play along: "When I heard the first Charlie Parker record, I knew that that was the direction." Eddie was working a factory job just out of high school when a friend convinced him to go to Sioux Falls, South Dakota, to play lead alto in a regionally traveling "territory" band with a repertoire of old-time music: "It was pretty 'out there.' They called me Dr. Jazz . . . Any time I had a little solo like a two-bar or four-bar pick, man, I'd play about six thousand notes in that space. And all the people would be out there doing schottisches, and I was killing dancers, and they would look at you real weird." Eddie, who toured the territory with Fats Carlson and His

Cats, played seventy-two one-nighters in a row. The group never got to Minneapolis but did play the northern metropolis of Fargo: "I thought we were in New York when we hit Fargo. No kidding, man, it looked so big."

The group started adding vocal arrangements a la Four Freshmen, called themselves the Continentals, and played the Midwest, starting in La Crosse, Wisconsin. They played nice clubs in Chicago and Las Vegas. Eddie met some players on the road who would become Twin Cities fixtures, including Maurice Turner, Hank Hazlett, Buddy Davis, and Jimmy Bowman. When Uncle Sam intervened in his career, Eddie did a two-year stint during the Korean Conflict stationed in Hawaii. He disliked the army, and he had what he called a "jazz attitude." He said, "The jazz attitude is like being just you and only the cats that are on the same level as you musically... You don't even talk to cats that can't play." When the band broke up, Eddie married and returned for a short-lived stay in Philadelphia. After he and his wife lost their day gigs as file clerks, he said to her, "Why don't we go to Minneapolis? I still have my GI Bill and I'll go to this radio announcing school, Brown Institute, and see what happens."

After a brief time on KDUZ in Hutchinson, Minnesota, Eddie came to the Twin Cities. "First we played Vic's," said Eddie. "Vic Levine had a place, which was a hip place, and he saw us play in La Crosse and he came down and said, 'Man, we've got to have your band in Minneapolis.' That was the first time we got to Minneapolis." At one session Eddie met Duke Page, who told him Gary Berg was leaving Augie's and Eddie could have the job. Eddie recalled, "We'd do a half-an-hour bit and then play for one stripper for fifteen minutes, and that was the show."

Sundays were off nights in those days, and they provided a chance to go around town where "sessions" were happening, including at the Hoop-D-Doo on Nicollet. Berger recalled, "I went every Sunday night to the Hoop-D-Doo, because all the cats were playing there, man—Dave Karr, Bobby Kunin, Bobby Crea, and Bob Davis was playing piano. So we'd go down and sit in with those cats to try and get some credentials by sitting in with the best players around town."

Sessions didn't happen just on Sundays. The Blue Note on West Broadway had Monday sessions beginning at 10 AM. Then, in the afternoon, the action moved to Big Al's at South Fifth Street and Thirteenth Avenue. Eddie was also working the Key Club on Washington Avenue at the time. Musicians included drummer Bill Hobbs, guitarist Bryce Robertson, and

Sessions abounded in the 1950s, and the Hoop-D-Doo in Minneapolis was a happening place. Regulars there included Bill Blakkestad on drums, saxman Bob Crea, bassist Stu Anderson, and pianist Bob Davis.

young pianist Bobby Lyle. Eddie was never sure what happened between Duke Page and Augie Ratner, but Eddie took over the band and, between Augie's and the Saddle, they backed strippers for seven and a half years.

While he played some gigs at the Artists' Quarter, Eddie said they were not very satisfying musically: "The people who were in there were just like they are around the Viking and at the Five Corners Saloon. I mean, all these really rowdy-dowdy, hard-core drunks. I never drank like these people, man. Like when I went downtown to drink, I had a coat on and a tie, and I was at the Brass Rail drinking and behaving myself in a place and never caused a scene."

When recorded music seriously started to replace live bands on the Avenue in 1969, a former stripper asked Berger to put a group together to play the Riverside Cafe. Despite the fact Eddie was down on playing anything but a few casual engagements, he accepted. Another young piano phenom, Bobby Peterson, and drummer Gene Piccalo joined him.

Soon another after-hours place, the Rainbow Gallery, opened, but Eddie and the group were lured away by the idea of a real nightclub job where they could play jazz and make twenty-five dollars a night. So they moved over to Williams Pub on the West Bank. "I couldn't believe just going into a nightclub with nothing else—no strippers or nothing—and just be able to get up and blow jazz music," said Berger. Williams Pub's owner Bill Warner stuck with the group, even with the small crowds on Mondays and Tuesdays. Eddie thought Warner liked jazz musicians because they were regular people, not show business folks. Eddie's first album, *Live at Williams Pub,* was recorded in 1974. Sunday gigs were added successfully: "Now I don't know if it was kind of a marathon thing that was going on, or if they dug it, or if it was trendy, or what the situation was, but... the joint was packed every Sunday night. We just had wall-to-wall people. Some of it was the jazz thing and some of it was the socializing. But we even used to run matinees down there on Friday and different days. But we had a lot of people coming in there, and Bill kind of dug it because I was like really crazy, man." Although the steady job scene was waning, Eddie managed to pick up one-nighters on a regular basis. Ill health made a respirator part of his regular stage equipment. He taught at the West Bank School of Music and played almost until his death in 2008.

Also on the Avenue near Fifth Street was a Moose club that hosted many of the bands working in the 1950s and '60s, according to saxophonist Jack Landin. What had been Vic's and the Dome in that same block morphed into the Jockey Club, the scene of at least one killing on lower Hennepin. Later yet, it became the Roaring Twenties, occasionally playing host to nationally known recording artists such as Don Goldie, Don Jacoby, and Billy Butterfield. As the Roaring Twenties, it also boasted one of the last incarnations of vaudeville, with dancers such as Teddy Qualls, as well as strippers, comedians, and a first-rate local jazz group headed by pianist Tommy Mustachio. Mustachio left the Twin Cities in the late sixties for Columbus, Ohio, to study court reporting. Perhaps those keyboard chops served him well on his day gig.

Gambling parlors, as well as strip clubs, dotted the Avenue. The Coconut Grove flourished over Brady's (later Schinder's newsstand) near Sixth Street, where you could "Walk up a flight and save a dollar." The Grove had a circular bar and fourteen-piece band with a chorus line of eight girls. Sleizer's near Eighth Street featured Stu Olson on baritone sax and, in his early playing days, Doc Evans on drums. The Poodle, also in that neck of the woods and next to the Cafe di Napoli, had numerous local players including pianist Tommy O'Donnell and Tiny Reichel, who played a blond Kay bass strung backwards that looked like a cello in the hands of the ample southpaw.

Because of the nature of the surroundings, the Avenue has produced many a tale, a few of them embellished over the years and some perhaps more fiction than fact. Stan Scott relayed a story from Bob Crea, the great sax and clarinet man who died in 1980. Bobby had just purchased his dream car, a new Cadillac, and was being picked up from his engagement at a Hennepin Avenue strip club. When he came out of the club with one of the strippers hanging on him, he saw his girlfriend take off in the Cadillac at high speed, hitting every parking meter on the street as she fled.

Drummer George Avaloz, who was in and out of town playing with Billy Eckstine in Chicago, among other choice gigs, remembered his time at the Saddle Bar with Crea: "I was really dedicated at that time. I'd be practicing downstairs, and all the girls would be walking around buck naked, and it didn't even bother me. I'd be down there tap, tap, tap, tap, tap, you know, and the beer bottles were coming down the chute and breaking." Avaloz recalled this Crea vignette: "He'd go in the bathroom [with] a cigarette and a cherry bomb, and he put the fuse inside the cigarette, and he'd put it behind the toilet. So we'd be up in the bandstand playing, and about two minutes later you'd hear this big 'Boom!', and this guy would come running outside with his pants down to his knees, and he wouldn't know what the heck was going on. Can you imagine trying to sit at the stool there and a bomb going off? Bob Crea was something else."

Stripper "DC" Current was working the Roaring Twenties near Fifth and Hennepin, and word went out that her boyfriend intended to come in that night and shoot her while she was doing her dance. So the five-piece band, larger than most in the strip joints, formed a semi-circle behind the dancers on stage. In the band were Tommy Mustachio on piano, Dentley

Jazz writer Tom Surowicz wrote of drummer George Avaloz, "Sitting in with legendary singer Billy Eckstine, at the South of the Border Key Club in Minneapolis in the 1950s, proved to be a big turning point in Avaloz's career. Eckstine dug his drumming, and encouraged the youngster to head for Chicago."

Haugesag on tenor, trombonist George Myers, Chuck Heinz on drums, and bassist Jay Goetting. Needless to say none of them wanted to be behind DC when the fireworks began, but an alert bouncer headed off the would-be shooter at the door. Jan Jacobson relates another incident from one of the Hennepin Avenue stage bars when a stripper did a dance on top of the spinet piano, fell inside, and "wiped out half the piano. Hammers went flying . . . Somebody wanted to come out with the *Hennepin Avenue Gazette;* it was a humorous place, really, and chops became well honed."

It was on Eddie Berger's first strip-club gig that a wild tenor player in town came to visit his wife, who was a stripper. He was packing heat, and he blew her off a bar stool in the next room. It was said that Bill Blakkestad caught every bullet with a rim shot and never missed a beat of the show.

Blakkestad stories abound. Here's just one example.

The party's over! Or so they thought. The annual New Year's Day party at Stan and Marian Haugesag's had been a huge success, and Stan, Marian, and Jack Coan were spending a few quiet moments when the phone rang. It was Joanie Blakkestad. "Heard you're having a party. We'll be right out." Bang! Marian stood with the receiver in her hand, hoping the Blakkestads wouldn't be able to find the house. When the doorbell rang, the Blakkestads brought in their small dog, a little cutie that immediately pooped on the living room rug. Joanie found the beer and opened one for each of them. When Marian announced that she needed to get to bed, Jack Coan told the Blakkestads to follow him to their home. He lost them almost immediately. Then the phone rang. "Jack, where's Billy?" Jack said, "He was in the car with you, Joanie." She said, "When I got home, the door was open and Billy was gone." The next day, Stan heard that Bill, who was in the Bloomington city jail, had fallen out of the car and landed in a snowbank, where he slept until dawn. Marian said she didn't insist they spend the night with the Haugesags "because they had brought their dog and left their year old baby at home!"

When Blakkestad was on his game, though, he was a first-rate drummer. He was once one of the most in-demand percussionists in the Twin Cities, having come up with the jazz crowd of the fifties, including Bob Davis, Stu Anderson, Dave Karr, Bob Crea, and Herb Pilhofer, plus a stint with the Stan Kenton band. He recorded an album with Kenton's mellophonium band at the Holiday Ballroom near Chicago in 1962. One

A pioneer in local race relations, Bob Benham's orchestra was a mixed-race band in 1941. Featuring Oscar Pettiford on bass, Joe Disch on trombone, pianist Harold "Popeye" Booker, and namesake Benham on drums, the group played Minneapolis's Red Feather until business interests pressured them out in what *DownBeat* referred to as a "dismal failure."

of his last gigs in the Twin Cities was with Brazilian pianist Manfredo Fest. He and Joanie lived in Las Vegas in the early seventies. Bill moved to Los Angeles, remarried, and ran a Montessori school. His body was said to have been discovered in his recreational vehicle, although the Los Angeles County coroner's office could shed little light on the circumstances or cause of death.

The Avenue claimed other establishments where jazz prevailed without the distraction of "dancers." One of them, on the lower end of Hennepin back in 1941, reported *DownBeat*, was a club near Fourth Street called the Red Feather. *DownBeat*'s review said, in the language of the time: "A mixed band, an unheard of innovation as far as Twin Citians are concerned, became a reality late last month when Bob Benham, local drummer, took over the bandstand at the Red Feather... Sepia stars who've had little chance to show their ability here in the last few years dominate the five-piece outfit of Benham's, with Harold (Popeye) Booker, the top Negro pianist in the northwest, Ira Pettiford, trumpet, Oscar Pettiford, bass, holding up the colored end of the group. A fine Minny trom man, Joe Disch, with drummer Benham and vocalist Barbara Bowron round out the outfit." Less than three years later, the Red Feather would be threatened with a boycott by a major Twin Cities defense plant and its ten thousand workers. *DownBeat* reported that the club's integration experiment had ended in "dismal failure . . . The people who patronize the Red Feather were taken aback by the sight of these men playing together and complained vociferously . . . Minneapolis still takes its music by sight and not sound."

Drummer Louis Bellson also played the Red Feather. He had family in St. Paul. Joe Kimball, who played his first gig at the New Brighton Hotel in 1933, worked Murray's Red Feather stage bar with Al Arbor and his Country Gentlemen in the late 1930s, and violinist Cliff Brunzell brought a jazz-string hybrid to the club in the forties. (A second Red Feather, probably unrelated, operated in St. Paul on University Avenue where a very young Bobby Lyle played piano.)

Reflecting on another club's excursion into the variety show format in the mid-1960s, pianist Butch Thompson once said that the attempt appeared to be "an ill-fated and naive effort to bring something just a little classier to the notorious Hennepin Avenue club scene. There were to be no strippers [at the Roaring Twenties], just Doc Evans's seven-piece band and a changing cast of singers, dancers, and comedians. Inevitably, it wasn't long before the place began to drift toward its old entertainment policy. Apparently the Avenue's habitual clientele preferred derrieres to Dixieland." Today, lower Hennepin is a mix of historic buildings, redeveloped properties, and a few familiar names like Augie's, the Brass Rail, and the Gay '90s, but in the new millennium you'd be hard-pressed to hear a note of jazz wafting from an open doorway.

7

Twin Cities Jazz Celebs

"[Historians say] Minneapolis cannot lay claim to a defining jazz artist in the way New Orleans can claim Louis Armstrong or Kansas City can claim Charlie Parker. Here, the jazz historians are wrong."

—Max Sparber, *playwright*

The Twin Cities may rightfully lay claim to myriad fine jazz musicians. Many of them never left the confines of the twin towns. Others ventured out and returned. Still others made their homes in Minneapolis and St. Paul for some years or decades and then went on to fame and fortune, or obscurity or worse.

LESTER YOUNG (1909–59)

Tenor saxophonist and clarinetist Lester Young, one of jazz's finest, most influential players, spent the better part of a decade (1926–36) in Minneapolis. Biographer Douglas Daniels asserts that "Minneapolis stands out not only as the place where Lester Young adopted the tenor sax and developed his craft" but it is also where he "acquired his distinctive way of holding the instrument out to the side."

Young, born in Mississippi, was introduced to the world of professional performance at a very early age in the Young Family Band, also known as the Billy Young Jazz Band. Lester's father, Willis Handy Young, moved the family to a large house at 573 Seventh Avenue North in Minneapolis in 1919–20. A Minneapolis relative may have helped coax them to the area, but another likely hypothesis is simply that Willis wanted to distance his family from the racially charged Jim Crow South. The band toured on the road, mostly in the Midwest, in the early twenties. It appears that it played its first Twin Cities–area gig on November 1, 1925, and then hit the road again in April 1926. Minnesota winters were a new phenomenon for the players.

Band trumpet player Leonard Phillips said, "I'll never forget it. When we went to play, we never saw the ground. There was snow up there. So, we went in and played the dance, and everything was packed and everything was nice." He remembered that Lester's father "already had this big house rented up there in Minneapolis for all the musicians. Some people who'd been on the show before, he knew them, were taking care of the house. All of us stayed in one room, Lester, Pete Jones, and I, so we had a good time playing, good food to eat. There was a big room where we'd rehearse practically every day. We didn't have a job right after that one. We made ten dollars, which was a lot of money then, for that night."

Lester and "Phil" Phillips attended grammar school in Minneapolis along with Lester's younger sister, Irma, and his brother, Lee. Lester became an avid record collector in Minneapolis, something that helped hone his style and sound. Once the band had established a firm base in the area, it did less traveling. That meant hearing fewer bands, so records became a more important music resource. By the winter of 1926–27, a lot more jazz was making it on to 78-rpm discs, and newly utilized microphones rendered a better sound. At home in Minneapolis, the trio of Pete Jones, Phil Phillips, and Lester Young would make its way to the record shop almost daily to preview discs. The three bought a few each time and built up a good-sized collection.

The Young Family Band evolved into an eleven-piece big band known as the New Orleans Strutters. It was booked into the Radisson and St. Paul hotels along with other Twin Cities locations. The South Side Ballroom, a black and tan club near Washington Avenue at Minneapolis's Seven Corners, provided another venue. It was there that they played and sang such current favorites as "Ain't She Sweet," "Five Foot Two," "Tiger Rag," and a lot of waltzes. The band became one of the most in demand in the Twin Cities and virtually the only one of that size.

Lester's brother Lee Young remembered the band's early days in Minneapolis: "That was probably the best band there was in Minneapolis . . .

[Willis] had a chance to go on the Orpheum circuit [but] they wanted him to cut two men out of the band. He was a high-principled man, and he would not. Everybody was just dying to get on the Orpheum circuit, you know, that was the biggest thing that you could do in Vaudeville then." Lee said the band then "continued to do those little one-nighters up in Bismarck, North Dakota, you know, Devils Lake. They used to play all over the Dakotas, but I quit traveling with them during school. I used to be the vocalist in the band, so during school I would remain in Minneapolis, and my dad and Lester would go out on the road."

Leonard Phillips noted the absence of racial segregation in Minneapolis: "Both black and white people would come and listen. The wife of the piano player [Gurvis Oliver] was white, and so was the drummer's [Ben Wilkerson's] wife. Nobody shared the bill with Young's group. He had the whole show by himself." Phillips said Lester played all the improvised solos and snuck in the blues, which he loved, whenever possible. Other musicians in the band included Ray Jones on banjo, Otto "Pete" Jones on trombone, the elder Young on tuba, and Phillips and Arthur Williams on trumpets. The band played from late 1926 until January 1928, when Lester and Phillips quit and left the Twin Cities to play with Art Bronson's Bostonians. Phillips had high respect for Willis Young: "Lester's father had a big influence in Minneapolis. He could go anywhere and get what he wanted. He gave me a Buescher trumpet for Christmas, a pretty one, too. Most of everybody in there had Bueschers but the C-melody saxophones were Conns."

Lester Young and Iowa-born Eddie Barefield became fast friends while sharing hotel accommodations in Bismarck, North Dakota, in 1927. Their mutual interest in listening to phonograph records at every opportunity expanded the friendship. They went their separate ways but hooked up again in Minneapolis in 1929 and formed an unusual alto and tenor sax duo.

It was in Minneapolis that Lester developed his trademark stance, holding the saxophone at an uncomfortable-appearing angle away from his right side. He started playing "tricks" in his father's band, notably on "Tiger Rag." "It was his number, and we played it way up in tempo, too," said Phillips. "He played the horn upside down when he made all the breaks, and then, when we got to the trio part and got back to the chorus again, he put it behind him and made the breaks in behind him. He'd break the house up when he did that, because you would not see it done like that. He used that trick with anybody he played with at that time, [including] King Oliver and the Blue Devils."

About six feet tall with a light complexion, auburn hair, and greenish eyes, Lester Young was sometimes called "Red," though he darkened his hair and conked or straightened it. He later became known for his deadpan demeanor and a unique hipster language all his own that even those close to him struggled to learn. But he wasn't known as "Prez" until Billie Holiday laid that moniker on him nearly two decades later, and Eddie Barefield remembers the twenty-two-year-old Young as "pretty straight. He hadn't developed that strange way of talking . . . he was quiet, very talented . . . didn't curse, or drink even." Lee Young supports that memory, saying, "No one in our family ever drank or smoked." This monastic lifestyle was short lived, though, and Lester's escapades into drugs and alcohol became well known later in his life. He also developed a sharp tongue, with expletives peppering his famous hipster talk.

Lee Young described his brother's alto playing as "running a lot of scales . . . he used to run all over the horn a lot," but he said Lester's style on the tenor was "more mellow—he did change considerably." Benny Carter, a great jazz alto saxophonist as well as a trumpeter and composer, heard Young playing alto in Minneapolis around 1931 and supported Lee Young's assertion that Lester was flashier on alto than tenor: "When I was on the road with McKinney's Cotton Pickers . . . we hit Minneapolis, and somebody told us about a wonderful alto player in a local club. I went to hear Prez and was enraptured. It was the greatest thing I'd ever heard. He had a definition and a mastery that I don't think he ever felt necessary to display on the tenor." Saxophonist Budd Johnson said McKinney's group offered Young a job if he would play alto all the time, but he declined. In the early thirties Lester played briefly again for the family band, but when they packed up and moved to the Southwest, Lester moved on to Eli Rice's Cotton Pickers.

In 1930, Lester lived in downtown Minneapolis with Bess Cooper, whom he married, and they had a daughter, Beverly. Bess died tragically soon afterward, and Young rarely spoke of Beverly, but he kept in touch with her at her home in St. Louis Park. In an interview for Bruce Freidricksen's documentary film about Lester titled *Song of the Spirit*, Beverly said, "He really cared about my mother. Her death really dug a hole in his heart."

For a time Lester lived with Leroy White and his family in a large house in Minneapolis, where the players had frequent jam sessions. Young boasted to Phil Phillips, "I can play a hundred choruses and play different for every chorus!" Phillips said Young "jammed there so much and played there for himself with just piano and drums. That was in 1930 and '31 when he played with Frank Hines. Lester said, 'When you play by yourself you can do that, because different ideas come to you.'"

During his years in the Twin Cities, Lester played at the Nest in North Minneapolis with such notables as Frank Hines, Eddie Barefield, and Leroy "Snake" White. He played Eugene Schuck's Cotton Club in 1931 as well as with Paul Cephas at the South Side Club.

According to Frank Büchmann-Møller's biography *You Just Fight for Your Life*, Young made brief road trips outside the Twin Cities in the early thirties with Frank Hines, the Original Blue Devils, and King Oliver. In February 1934 Lester briefly joined Count Basie's Cherry Blossoms in Kansas City. Some touring in the early thirties with King Oliver and the Bennie Moten–George E. Lee Band kept him mostly in the country's midsection, and it gave him a chance to be heard by Basie and even play a handful of gigs with him. Those years, however, were devoted mostly to playing around the Twin Cities.

Club manager Pete Karalis knew talent when he saw it. In 1934, police closed down Minneapolis's notorious Apex Club, whose band featured Rook Ganz, Popeye Booker, Adolphus Alsbrook, Bill Pew, and Harry Pettiford. "It struck me this group would be unemployed," said Karalis, "so I decided to sign them to a contract even though I didn't have a place for them to play. I did have a place in mind, though." Karalis brought Boyd Atkins up from Chicago to front the group and write arrangements at the El Patio in St. Louis Park. Karalis said, "I sold the idea to the four Greek boys at the club. I then auditioned the group with Bob DeHaven and Lee Whiting at WTCN. They really liked the group and said they'd give me a line out there for thirty-nine dollars a month. I spent the remainder of my capital on paint to write 'Cotton Club' on the roof. We had a fairly good dinner trade, and the boys were proud of their restaurant . . . The group used to play the dinner shift. Boyd had arranged some things." Karalis then replaced Pettiford with Lester, to whom he sent a ticket in Kansas City, where he had been playing.

Besides being a great jazz musician, Karalis said, Lester was, "one of the gentlest, nicest human beings I'd ever met." Karalis boasted of the band's lyricism and drive. Longtime Twin Cities saxman Percy Hughes said, "There was happiness in Lester's playing, a little comedy, and all of a sudden a little roughness." The entire band made $126 a week. Lester's daughter Beverly observed that since there was no money to be made in the Twin Cities, "you did it for the love of playing."

From June 1935 to February 1936 Lester Young and Rook Ganz were back playing at the Cotton Club. The place was clean, neat, well run, and without rough stuff. It was the more established and familiar Minneapolis musician Rook Ganz whom people came to hear. George Putnam, later with Pathe News, was the radio announcer. Longtime Twin Cities reedman Dick Pendleton recalled that the musicians were "friendly as they could be." Lester would leave the bandstand for some of his solos in order to stroll and serenade the diners at their tables and booths. When Pendleton asked him for lessons, Lester said, "I'd like to help you but I got a telegram from a man from Kansas City that wants me to join the band."

Lester recounted how that move came about: "I was playing at the Cotton Club in Minneapolis. I used to hear the Count on his broadcasts when I was off from work . . . Everything was fine with the band but the tenor player. I sent Basie a telegram and asked him if he could use a tenor player. I was in my twenties by this time. He'd heard of me because people had gone up to Minneapolis for various shows, and Minneapolis was the winter quarters for the band."

About Lester's playing at the Cotton Club, Pendleton remembered peering into an open window to watch: "I never heard anybody that played so loose—it just flows; breathy. He didn't change very much. All the musicians admired him." Boyd Atkins's arrangements were said to be top-notch and very soulful. Other players like trombonist Jerry Mullaney and saxophonists Frankie Roberts and Ray Kammerer, whom locals considered the best around, would join in and exchange choruses with Lester Young. Young's daughter Beverly said, "He stayed here as long as he could."

Lester left town and never returned except for short visits. Minneapolis saxophonist Morris Wilson recalls running into Lester by chance on the Near Northside at the time of Lester's last performance in Minneapolis as a member of a Jazz at the Philharmonic tour in the early 1950s. For a quarter century, Prez played with most of the great jazz musicians, traveled a lot, and spent time in Europe. Ailing after his last trip, he called Beverly to New York, where she visited with him at the Alvin Hotel before his death in 1959.

ADOLPHUS ALSBROOK (1921–88)

Double-bassist Adolphus Alsbrook was a fascinating, highly respected musician who spent most of the years from 1933 to 1954 in the Twin Cities. Players considered him a tremendous all-around talent. He read well; he played well; he knew all the instruments in the orchestra. Besides the bass, for which he was best known, he played harp.

Oscar Pettiford, another great bassist, considered Alsbrook one of his major influences: "I was impressed by [Jimmy] Blanton and by Adolphus Alsbrook, a Minneapolis bassist I'd known since I was about sixteen in 1938. He was one who was really playing the instrument." Alsbrook played with Duke Ellington's band briefly in 1939, but it didn't work well for either the bandleader or the bassist, who didn't like the road. Alsbrook was said to be one of the few to ever quit Duke's band. Shortly thereafter, Blanton signed on. Alsbrook's son Darryl later said that his father left Duke only because he could make more money arranging, that his father deeply regretted leaving Duke, and that the only time he ever saw his father cry was when Duke died.

Paul de Barros wrote in *Jackson Street After Hours* that Alsbrook was "a great bass player, but he complained that Duke was using all the wrong chords. He was a great arranger, too, but he didn't want to consider that Duke was creating a new sound in music. Alsbrook became a professor up at the University of Minnesota." Alsbrook also played short stints with Count Basie and Thelonious Monk. This mention of Alsbrook's professorial credentials could be challenged, although Alsbrook was a well-read man and able to talk about any current topic. He attended the University of Kansas, the University of Minnesota, and the Chicago Conservatory, but he had no degree despite credits all over the place. He would take courses that interested him and for a time taught judo to Minneapolis police officers.

Alsbrook's talent and plight caught the attention of Don Lang, who wrote in *DownBeat* in the 1940s: "One of the Northwest's finest colored musicians, Adolphus Ahlsbrook *[sic]*, bass man with Boyd Atkins' old Cotton Club band, who worked with Duke Ellington, a U of Minn. grad and arranger for the best bands to hit the Twin Cities, is now clerking in a drug store and trying to get on the Minneapolis police force in order to make a living." Lang continued with comments on the challenges for musicians playing jazz in the city: "The situation for Negro musicians here is terrible. Ahslbrook and nearly all the others play only jobbing dates about once in two or three months. The Cotton Club was the last Minneapolis spot to employ a colored band. The only spice left for these musicians is the after hour jam session, now fading out of the picture with . . . blue-noses prowling the Twin City alleys at night."

When Alsbrook first arrived in Minneapolis in the fall of 1933, he had already played with Count Basie and King Oliver. Alsbrook said he "told King I'd like to leave the band now—'Do I have to give two weeks' notice?' Oliver said, 'No, if you like to leave, go ahead and leave. You're not going to do me any good if you're playing against your will.' I left King Oliver August 24. I told these guys I'm ready to go. They said we're going to go see Paul [Webster] in Minneapolis and then we're going to go to the World's Fair in Chicago and then we're going back home. I stayed in Minneapolis." Alsbrook played at Howard's Steak House at Sixth Avenue North and Lyndale, one of the most renowned of the after-hours hangouts for jazz musicians. In 1944 drummer Bill Blakkestad put together sessions with Alsbrook, pianist Popeye Booker, and saxman Eric Giere. Julian Henson remembers working with Alsbrook at the Rhumboogie Club in Minneapolis in the 1940s.

In the Twin Cities, Alsbrook played with the all-star group, including Lester Young and Rook Ganz at the El Patio in St. Louis Park. Jo Jones would show up to sit in for drummer Gene Reid. Lester had replaced Harry Pettiford based partially on Alsbrook's recommendation. Ganz told Alsbrook he had heard about Lester but never heard him play, and the bassist said not to worry about it. Ganz asked, "What about his reading?" Alsbrook said, "Well, he read King Oliver's music." Ganz replied, "Looks good enough for me." Pete Karalis then had Rook ask Lester to come to Minneapolis, tell him how much the job paid, and request he bring his wife and furniture. He had the job.

Alsbrook, a much-underrated bassist, received special mention in Charles Mingus's autobiography, *Beneath the Underdog,* in this exchange between Mingus and Charlie "Bird" Parker. Bird said, "The other night I heard a cat play bass the way Adolphus Allbrook *[sic]* used to. It don't supposed to be possible but they do it." Mingus replied, "Bird, you putting me on? That's the second time I heard about Adolphus Alsbrook. Jimmy Blanton told me he carved a wooden pick with one hand, kept playing with the other, finished his pick, and played more than a guitar with it." Bird said, "Stone genius, Mingus . . . [He's] a scientist too—physics major. Teaches judo at the police department. Mastered the harp in two years." Another player said of Alsbrook, who was five-feet-ten and weighed well over two hundred pounds: "You didn't mess with him."

Former principal bassist in the Minneapolis Symphony Ray Fitch recalled that Alsbrook "had fantastically large and strong hands. He would be the envy of any bass man. He was smart and studied his lesson. He usually took the streetcar out to our house. On hot summer days, he used an umbrella to fend off the sun, and would show up with the umbrella in one hand and a bag of chocolate chip cookies in the other. I would have a cookie, then enjoy hearing him play his lesson. He always had it prepared." Fitch continued, "Adolphus was a gambler. He shot craps with his Cotton Club buddies, so he was always broke. Sometimes he would call and say he couldn't come for his lesson because he lost his money gambling. I would say, 'Come anyway and pay when you can.' When he won with the dice, he would call me and say, 'Mr. Fitch, I am mailing you fifteen dollars for future lessons. You keep it so I won't lose it.'" Fitch said they talked "about his plans for a career. 'There's no use in me studying serious classical music, because they'd never take me in any symphony,' he said. I had to agree with him at the time . . . Mother and I went over and heard him play several times at the Cotton Club . . . He was one of the best bass talents ever."

Dirk Fischer, a musician, educator, and brother of keyboardist Clare Fischer, said that Alsbrook "was a person who had studied legitimate harmony and all those academic ends of the music . . . I'd be coming home from my job out by Lake Harriet where I was closing up a hamburger joint and going to school in the daytime, and I'd meet him downtown, and we were all going over north. Adolphus would be carrying his bass on his back, and we'd be standing on the corner of Hennepin . . . waiting for a trolley and it's thirty degrees below zero, and we're talking music theory." One time they got on the trolley and, to their surprise, trumpeter Don Charleston was driving. He "upset all the customers by demanding that Adolphus pay for a seat for his bass." Fischer noted that Adolphus "wrote for Rudy Vallee for years and harp music and others . . . He was writing for the Lawrence Welk Show, but they let him go. His arrangements swung too much." Alsbrook, who suffered from narcolepsy, said, "I used to go everyplace on the streetcar or bus. See I can't drive . . . I fall asleep easy." That included on the bandstand, but colleagues said he'd wake up and be right on the beat.

While Alsbrook lived in the Twin Cities for many years, he spent at least twenty months in Seattle in 1945–47 and a brief stint in Kansas City. Writer Brian Priestly said Alsbrook worked regularly on the West Coast before going up to the Seattle area, where local musicians remember him playing in the late 1940s. Howard Rumsey, who ran the famous Lighthouse jazz club in Southern California, said that Alsbrook—a fine musician, quiet, and a gentleman—played briefly around Los Angeles. Musician Gerald Wiggins recalled that he played with Alsbrook at the Velvet Turtle in Los Angeles in the forties. British trumpeter and writer John Chilton, who tried to interview Alsbrook by phone but found him very uncooperative, or perhaps disillusioned, wrote, "People like Red Callender certainly confirmed his existence, though not necessarily Mingus's high opinion of him."

Alsbrook moved to Los Angeles in 1954 and went on to record with Sam Cooke and other pop and R&B groups, and he did some writing for television. He became a member of American Federation of Musicians Local 145 in Vancouver. Fred Stride, a Canadian musician, recounted, "I had the fortune to play with him only once [around 1979–80]. I remember him as a classy person. He was also the first bass player I ever worked with who didn't use an amp." Since Alsbrook was very modest about his skills, his son Darryl Alsbrook was surprised to learn about his dad's professional history, on the Internet. Alsbrook died in Canada on June 2, 1988.

OSCAR PETTIFORD (1922–60)

In a recent radio chat with Marian McPartland on NPR's *Piano Jazz*, the great bassist Ron Carter noted the resurgence of interest in Oscar Pettiford, a jazz master with deep roots in the Twin Cities. The duo of Carter and McPartland then performed "Blues in the Closet" and talked extensively about "Tricrotism," two of the jazz standards penned by Pettiford.

Like Lester Young, Oscar and his talented siblings grew up in a family band in the Twin Cities. Oscar was born in Okmulgee, Oklahoma, in 1922 to his Choctaw Indian mother and Cherokee–African American father. His father, known as "Doc" Pettiford because he was a veterinarian, formed a family band in the 1920s. Oscar's mother, who played in the band, taught theory and harmony to the eleven Pettiford children, although Ira Pettiford's wife, Jeanne, later said, "Nobody was taught anything. If they needed a trumpet player, someone shoved it in your face, said 'We're going to play a gig tonight,' and handed everybody a horn."

Oscar was three years old and living in Minneapolis when the family band began touring the Midwest and the South. Dizzy Gillespie recalled, "I remember the Doc Pettiford family. They'd come through my hometown [Cheraw, South Carolina] when I was a kid." (Oscar would go on to play with Dizzy Gillespie's quintet at New York's Onyx Club in 1943.) Another early account says Oscar was six years old and a dancer before he learned an instrument. He told writer Robert Reisner, "I got started at six when I used to dance with my father's band. When I was seventeen, I had a bit role with Olsen and Johnson in Minneapolis. Before I settled on bass, I played piano, trombone, and trumpet, which hurt my jaws, and I studied tailoring in case the music business got tough." He even fronted the band on occasion and, at age ten, played drums. He added baton twirling and finally became a bassist at fourteen.

George Hoefer said in a *DownBeat* article that after Oscar's father "brought in an outsider to play bass horn in 1930, he really started to pay attention to the band. Young Oscar then began playing trumpet and trombone in addition to drums and piano. The bass horn player got married and left the band in 1936, and Oscar... stepped in his place. This happened in Augusta, Georgia, where the band was on summer location. A musician named Kid Chocolate... had left his bass in the storage room of the place where they were working, and Oscar started on that. When Chocolate came back, Oscar's dad bought him his own bass."

Oscar was proud of his large family's talents. He told writer Nat Hentoff that he heard Dizzy Gillespie and Charlie Parker before he left Minneapolis but he considered his brother Harry Pettiford "one of the greatest saxophonists in the world." He also boasted about his sister Margie, but

Dizzy said Oscar tried "to make out that someone in the family was better than he, but he was the best in the family." In 1986, when broadcaster Leigh Kamman led a tribute to Pettiford at Minneapolis's Walker Art Center (part of the series *Bop Echoes,* which another great broadcaster, Billy Taylor, recorded for CBS's *Sunday Morning*), Dizzy Gillespie commented negatively about Oscar, especially about his tardiness to a recording date. Percy Hughes, Ken Green, Dave Faison, and others who heard Margie Pettiford contend she was a phenomenal sax player and likely the best musician in the talented Pettiford family.

Oscar or Helen may have been the youngest in the family. Oldest sister Leona played piano. She was followed by Ira, who played trumpet, and trombonist-drummer Alonzo, who played in Jay McShann's band until he contracted tuberculosis. Margie, five years older than Oscar, later joined the International Sweethearts of Rhythm, an integrated all-woman organization that had a sterling reputation for quality and swing. A nervous breakdown on the road followed by a lobotomy ended her career, and she was institutionalized until her death. Another Pettiford sister, Cecilia, was also a saxophone player. Like other siblings, she began drinking at a very early age to combat stage fright. She left the band but returned to it and had a family.

Oscar's brother Harry was a well-known and in-demand Twin Cities saxophonist. WLOL broadcaster Bob Bouchier said he "played a million notes," and then likened him and sister Margie to Charlie Parker. Rosemary and three other sisters sang. They all skipped school frequently after playing night gigs. "They had a rough life," said Ira's wife, Jeanne.

Oscar continued to perform with the family band after graduating from Minneapolis North High School. The band often played at Swing City, an all-ages club at St. Paul's northern city limits. A prominent attraction in their set was Pettiford's older sister Leontine, a pianist who doubled on reeds and contributed most of the arrangements. She left the band to marry a sax player.

Ken Green, who played piano at the time, first met the Pettifords at the 38 Club at Tenth and St. Peter in St. Paul and on Saturday afternoons beginning in 1933 at Curly's at Fifth and Hennepin in Minneapolis. "Ma and Pa" Pettiford played the Old Southern Barbecue at 700 Lyndale Avenue North, Ma on piano and Pa on drums. Nearby was the Just Right

Barbecue (said to have better ribs but no music). The Clef Club was up the block at 637 Lyndale in the Kistler Building on the third floor. The Pettifords lived across the street, later moving nearby to Seventh and Oak Lake.

Green said the very large Pettiford family probably had very little money: "The house was no showplace. I was over there eating lunch with Oscar, and his mother puts his plate down, and I said, 'What's that?' And she said, 'That's greens.' And I said, 'Oscar, greens, what's that?' He said, 'That's greens, man!' I said, 'Green what?' He said 'It's greens.' I said, 'Well, is it dandelion greens or pea greens or what kind of greens is it?' He said, 'Those are greens, man, you just eat them. They're good for you.'" Green said his own parents, like many people at the time, were mildly and mindlessly racist: "I'd bring Oscar over for lunch, and I could tell my folks were very uneasy about this."

Tenor saxophonist Tommy Bauer remembers going out with the Pettifords in their teen years on Rice Street in St. Paul. They couldn't get into the joints, but they wanted to learn to play jazz. "We'd hear Jimmy Lunceford or Chick Webb. From the front of the theater, we heard Ella. That did it right there," he declared. Nothing could stop Tommy, Ira, and Oscar from becoming musicians. Bauer noted there was nobody to teach them how to play jazz; in fact, teaching it was frowned upon, so they listened outside the clubs and to recordings of Kid Ory, Louis Armstrong, Jack Teagarden, and, Bauer's earliest influence, Frankie Trumbauer. Bauer spent time with Boyd Raeburn's band and can be heard on several significant recordings. Around this time Harry Pettiford turned down a chance to go with the Ellington band. Bauer said, "That was the real jazz coming up from Chicago, four beat, while Dixie was still two beat."

In early 1933, Oscar and Harry Pettiford joined Eli Rice and his Cotton Pickers band, a significant group on the Twin Cities scene. Arthur Goldberg and Frankie Roberts recalled the Cotton Pickers being among the first traveling black bands they saw in St. Paul in the twenties. The Pettiford family had worked with and for Eli as early as November 1931, overlapping with Boyd Atkins prior to his coming to Minneapolis at mid-decade.

David Bastien, son of bassist Ovid "Biddy" Bastien, called the Twin Cities "Bass Player Central" because of the towns' many fine bassists, then and now: "The Bastiens, the Hugharts, the Petersons, the Pettifords—

all have been important bass families, and there are a great many good young musicians here playing bass." David said Biddy "reminisced about the years around 1935 when jam sessions were *de rigueur* at the El Patio in St. Louis Park, the Pettiford family's restaurant in North Minneapolis [the Old Southern Barbecue], and an all-night jazz club at Tenth Avenue South and Washington in Minneapolis... It was here that Biddy learned to play 'real jazz.' Oscar and Ira were quite young at the time and they would listen. Biddy knew them as young 'hero worshippers' who were very interested in bass (especially in *his* bass playing)."

Oscar passed on the favor. Young bassist Dick Norling recalled, "Being able to go out and meet people like Oscar Pettiford and Ira... Oscar was so nice when I was starting out as a kid bass player. Oscar would say, 'Hey, Dick. Come on up.' I had all I could do to push the strings down because he had such a high action on his bass."

Jams at El Patio often turned into more than all-night affairs, according to drummer Bob Burns: "We started work at nine o'clock with a six-piece orchestra; at one o'clock, we cut down to three; by one-thirty, we'd have fifteen to twenty men on the stand, everybody blowin'. This was not only local musicians but, remember, it was the era of the big band: Benny Goodman, Tommy Dorsey, Jimmy Dorsey, Glenn Miller—men like that on the stand at the same time." Burns continued, "We'd work there until three o'clock in the morning, shut down, then go up north where Rook and the other fellas were playing. We'd stay there 'til eight, nine o'clock in the morning. If some of that music could have been recorded, I'm sure it would go down in the archives of history as some of the greatest ever performed."

By the mid-1930s Oscar Pettiford was attracting broad attention. He recalled a most flattering encounter: "One night Duke Ellington heard me at an after-hours jam session and approached me to join the band. That was before Blanton. But I was fourteen or fifteen and was breaking the law playing, as it was. So I couldn't join him. I did get to hear Blanton when I was about seventeen. When I heard him, I was in love with him right away." At sixteen, Oscar was introduced to Adolphus Alsbrook: "He was one who was really playing the instrument."

Seventeen-year-old Oscar also played at the Harlem Breakfast Club on Minneapolis's Near Northside in an after-hours jam-session setting. On September 24, 1939, between midnight and 4 AM, players there included Jerry Jerome, tenor sax; Charlie Christian, guitar; and Frankie Hines, piano. The engineer was Jerry Newhouse, who was responsible for earlier off-air recordings of the Benny Goodman orchestra for producer John Hammond. His ubiquitous recorder memorialized many a jam session and produced an impressive archive. Leigh Kamman called him a guide and mentor.

Newhouse and reed man Dick Pendleton picked up Christian and Jerome after their gig with Benny Goodman at the St. Paul Orpheum, and Newhouse recorded the Near Northside session using a Presto acetate disc recorder (12-inch, 78-rpm discs). *New Yorker* writer Whitney Balliett thought Christian was the standout of that session: "Christian stretches out and sounds as if he could play a hundred straight choruses without repeating a phrase." Some of the tunes from that session ("Star Dust," "I Got Rhythm," and "Tea for Two") were combined with others, solos spliced together, and released by Columbia as *Solo Flight: The Genius of Charlie Christian*. It was Pettiford's first recording and still survives today. (Many air checks released on LP and CD from that era have come from the Newhouse archives.)

After seeing Balliett's reference to the session and objecting to being called a "disc jockey," Newhouse attempted to set the record straight for Balliett: "Thanks very much, but I was *not* a disc jockey—just one of the world's greatest living authorities on jazz who was occasionally invited to sound off on the air. The correct date was in the week of September 21, 1939." He continued, "Benny and the band were playing a week's run at the St. Paul Orpheum Theatre. The impromptu recording session took place after-hours at the Harlem Breakfast Club in Minneapolis. The personnel were as you've listed it except that the bassist was Oscar Pettiford, and there was *no* drummer."

It was also in 1939 that Oscar first met Jimmy Blanton, who came through Minneapolis with the Ellington band. Said Oscar, "I was just with him one night. We had a head-cutting contest right away. Our approaches were a lot alike. We hung out from early evening to break of day. If he'd stayed alive, I'd probably still be in Minneapolis."

In the same year, Oscar left the family band briefly for a small role with the Olsen and Johnson show in a Minneapolis theater. The vaudevillians launched their famous show, "Hellzapoppin," the year before. Oscar then returned to play with his family until 1941. That summer Ken Green, drummer Sid Smith, and Oscar Pettiford went to Mitch's in Mendota to

Eddie Tolck appeared at all the name clubs around the Twin Cities in the late thirties and forties. Often seen as a drummer, Tolck was playing vibes at Mitch's in Mendota when Oscar Pettiford, Ken Green, and Sid Smith went to hear the Doc Evans–Harry Blons band in 1941.

hear Doc Evans, Harry Blons, and Eddie Tolck on vibes. Rufus Webster, an accomplished keyboardist and later a Minneapolis school administrator, said Oscar had gone far in his development, and even more so after he went to New York. Jimmy Blanton and Oscar Pettiford were the only ones who played in that emerging pre-bebop style that made the bass an accepted solo instrument. Writer-critic Ira Gitler noted that Oscar played with clarity. Dick Katz said he was "the closest thing to Charlie Christian that we've had." Another aspect of Oscar's style was to insert musical quotes from nursery rhymes and other familiar tunes. Ken Green said Oscar played advanced bass even before he left Minneapolis.

Throughout the late thirties and early forties, according to Green, Bar Harbor in Nisswa, north of Brainerd, Minnesota, was the "big carouse" for kids, but when wartime gas rationing took effect, Bob Smith opened Har Barbor, what he called "the poor man's Nisswa," on Lake Minnetonka near Minneapolis. The club featured the Pettifords, Rufus Webster, and other Twin Cities musicians. When the Pettiford Family Band finally broke up in 1941, Oscar joined Bob Benham's quartet in Minneapolis. He also worked with other local groups, one of which included his brother Ira.

It was at this time that broadcast legend Leigh Kamman hitchhiked to Duluth and won a broadcasting audition at WEBC. Kamman introduced Coleman Hawkins to Oscar just before the WEBC program *Symphony in Riffs,* which aired Saturdays at 11 PM from the legendary and classy Flame in Duluth. As they were doing level checks one Saturday afternoon, Hawkins, who had a ten-day engagement there, asked Pettiford to play something. Pettiford had mastered Jimmy Blanton's "Jack the Bear," and he could play it as skillfully as Jimmy did. When he then played "Pitter Panther Patter," Hawkins was absolutely impressed. "Why don't you sit in with us tonight on the broadcast," he suggested. Afterward, they jammed until dawn back at the studio. Kamman said they recorded that night, but the 16-inch acetates didn't survive. Pettiford and Hawkins became fast friends and later played in Europe together.

Perhaps the most widely told tale about Oscar Pettiford in the Twin Cities dates to an afternoon in 1941 at Coffman Memorial Union on the University of Minnesota campus. It was a meeting of the new Boogie-Woogie Club. Oscar and his colleagues Ken Green and Sid Smith talked Dmitri Mitropoulos, conductor of the Minneapolis Symphony Orchestra, into attending. The *Minneapolis Star Journal* reported the gathering on March 11, 1941, when three thousand students jammed into the grand ballroom of the union to hear a tune two students had written in Mitropoulos's honor while the conductor had to sit on the floor. When a seven-piece band swung into "Beat Me, Dmitri" with a boogie-woogie beat, the students "clapped hands, stomped, and cried, 'Scrub me, momma.'" Mitropoulos smiled, then frowned, then shook his head.

Outside Coffman Memorial Union on the University of Minnesota campus, March 1941, some of the top players of the day gathered: front row, left to right, Doc Evans, Rook Ganz, Dale Olinger, Ira Pettiford, Tom Morgan; back row, Popeye Booker, pianist; Eddie Tolck, drums; Oscar Pettiford, bass. A very young Leigh Kamman holds the microphone on the right.

After the band had beat out the last bar, Green, one of the song's composers, "undertook to explain boogie-woogie to the maestro," while Sid Smith, his collaborator, stood by. "It's eight beats to the bar," Green said. "The left hand does a walking bass while the right hand improvises." Mitropoulos protested, "It's monotonous—funny music is only funny when you play it seriously. Otherwise it is no good." Following that infamous encounter, Smith, Green, and Joe Reichman, known as the "Pagliacci of the Piano," were hired to play the Minneapolis Orpheum Theatre, where Kamman also served as emcee. (Mitropoulos did gain a modest affinity for boogie-woogie. In an article in *Life* magazine on February 18, 1946, Mitropoulos said he spent parts of his summers helping with Red Cross blood drives, "occasionally varying his routine by playing boogie-woogie on farmhouse pianos while their owners' veins were being tapped." Some symphony supporters protested, saying that this was a violation of their cultural values. Ray Fitch said Mitropoulos didn't play much jazz. His feelings toward jazz were "colored grey" because of its association with overindulgence.)

After World War II began in 1941, Oscar Pettiford got a job in a defense plant for six months. "You could starve to death trying to play in Minneapolis," he said. That prompted legendary bassist Milt Hinton to say, "No way... You have to play. Man, don't let that talent go down the drain. There isn't anybody here playing like you, and you could more than hold your own in New York City." Ken Green commented: "There was Oscar in the wilds of the jazz jungle, and Milt took him under his wing." The young bassist had become so discouraged with the prospects for playing music in his hometown that he briefly quit the profession altogether.

Despite trying conditions, Oscar's reputation continued to grow. Frank Büchmann-Møller wrote in his biography of saxophonist Ben Webster that, "On March 18, 1937, [Cab] Calloway's orchestra began a four-month tour... One evening after the show, during their stay in Minneapolis, [Milt] Hinton and Ben went to a nightclub in St. Paul where they heard a fourteen-year-old bassist named Oscar Pettiford. They were so impressed that they invited him to the theater the next day to let the other musicians from Calloway's band hear his gifted playing." When Oscar dropped by, Milt took him up to the rehearsal hall and organized a jam session. Hinton said, "He played, and Cab came up and heard him and fired me! I said, 'That's the last time I ever do that!' He wanted to hire Oscar right then and there, and kick me out. Oscar wouldn't go. Later on, he went with Duke."

In early 1943, Oscar made the move that would finally cut his ties to the Twin Cities. He joined the Charlie Barnet Orchestra, which included Chubby Jackson on bass. According to trumpeter Howard McGhee, Jackson was on the verge of getting fired. Oscar wrote "Concerto for Two Basses" and helped Jackson keep his job a while longer. From 1945 to 1948 Oscar played with the Duke Ellington orchestra. He went on to perform and record with the best in the business, sparking critics on both sides of the Atlantic—Leonard Feather in the United States and Hugues Pannasie in France—to dub Oscar Pettiford "the greatest bass player in the world." Pettiford took up residence in Europe and died in Copenhagen on September 8, 1960.

IRA PETTIFORD (c. 1916–82)

Oscar Pettiford's younger brother Ira was well known among the Twin Cities musicians with whom he played from the 1940s to well into the 1960s. Ira started out, of course, in the Pettiford Family Band and soon became well known among the players at Howard's Steak House, other Near Northside hangouts, and the El Patio in St. Louis Park. "We kept up to date," said Pettiford of the Boyd Atkins group that played at the club. "Boyd wrote the arrangements. We'd rehearse and every week we'd have a new bunch of tunes . . . We used to pack the El Patio in. They had wonderful crowds out there." Ira went on the road for a time with Benny Carter's band in 1946–47 but decided he'd rather be in the Twin Cities. Bassist Dave Faison said a factor in Ira's decision was his bandmates' constant needling about his pretty wife, Jeanne, at home. Faison remembered Ira in the 1948 group at Howard's, and in 1955 Ira played at the downtown Minneapolis Key Club with Eric Giere on sax and Bill Blakkestad, considered one of the finest drummers around.

Growing up as a multi-instrumentalist, Ira was also well known as a bassist. Although he sometimes even played guitar, it was the trumpet where he excelled. He was a high-register specialist who always played in good taste. Vic's was the site of the all-star group made up of Lester Young, Bill Boone, and Ira. They were occasionally joined by pianist Fritz Jones, known later as Ahmad Jamal. Ira is also known to have played session clubs Lee and Eddie's and Al Sperling's in the early fifties, as well as later gigs with Herb Schoenbohm's Brazilian-flavored group at Valli Pizza in the university campus's Dinkytown area. In 1958, Ira wrote an entertainment column called "The Cat's Corner" for the *Twin Cities Observer.* He continued to play around the Twin Cities into the 1960s and died in 1982.

FRANK MORGAN (1933–2007)

In the early fifties, when Leigh Kamman asked Charlie Parker to name some up-and-coming jazz artists, his short list included the young alto saxophonist Frank Morgan. Unfortunately, Morgan's life paralleled Bird's in some dangerous ways, but he managed to turn it around and live out his life in Minneapolis, where he was born. Morgan's father, Stanley, had been a guitarist for the Ink Spots, a popular vocal group in the 1930s and 1940s, and it was on the road that young Frank met Parker: "I met Bird after the show and told him I wanted to learn how to play one of those things." Parker encouraged Frank to start playing clarinet.

Morgan's family did not like living in the Twin Cities and moved to Milwaukee when Frank was seven. As a teen he was playing professionally in California, but he developed an addiction and served prison time in his early twenties. For the next several decades, he spent more time in prison than out. In San Quentin, he formed an all-star group that included fellow sax player and addict Art Pepper. Finally clean, Morgan recorded "Easy Livin'" in 1985 to much critical acclaim. After having a stroke in 1998, he recovered and in 2005 moved back to the Twin Cities, where he continued a scaled-back music schedule. It included a gig at the Dakota Jazz Club with Irv Williams and a series of duo concerts with local pianists. Morgan died on December 14, 2007, in Minneapolis after returning from a European tour.

SERGE CHALOFF (1923–57)

Regarded by many as jazz's preeminent baritone sax player in the late 1940s, Serge Chaloff spent a portion of his addiction-burdened life in the Twin Cities. One of the original Four Brothers in the Woody Herman Herd of 1946–47, Chaloff left the band over disagreements with Herman and problems with drugs. He recorded with Oscar Pettiford in 1949 and returned to his hometown Boston in 1951.

Chaloff landed again in Minneapolis in mid-1953, according to Bob McCaffery, a pianist of some repute. "One Sunday afternoon, while I was sitting in at the Hoop-D-Doo, Serge Chaloff, the poll-winning baritone saxophonist... came into the club. He was scheduled to begin a two-week engagement at Vic's, another local club, later that week," wrote McCaffery. "He had arrived in town with only a drummer and needed to find a pianist and a bass player. Serge didn't play that day but stayed for several sets. At the end of the session he asked me and a local bass player, Dick Thompson, if we could make the gig at Vic's. We were both flattered and immediately accepted. I was pretty sure that Serge had already been rejected by both [Lou] Levy and [Dave] Frishberg, but that didn't bother me." The group had one rehearsal at the union hall, which at that time was located on Glenwood Avenue just north of downtown Minneapolis. To McCaffery's delight, they played standards and tunes he knew, but "some tempos were furious and difficult to sustain. We played 'Four Brothers' at a frantic tempo." McCaffery called Chaloff "tolerant" but after a week, he and Thompson were replaced by Lou Levy and Stu Anderson. "This was an ego deflator, but we managed to rationalize it because our successors were significantly better players," he said.

McCaffery maintained a cordial relationship with Chaloff, who befriended local singer Dell Scott and sat in when and where he could. "On several occasions he called me in the early evening to accompany him on club-hopping ventures," said McCaffery. "I can still recall a stoned Serge driving Dell's car erratically as we made the rounds of Minneapolis clubs to sit in for free drinks." Saxophonist and disc jockey Dick LeMire said that one night Chaloff threw his horn into Lake Calhoun in a fit of disgust.

Chaloff played in October 1953 at the Flame Bar in downtown St. Paul after drummer Mel Leifman introduced Chaloff to Pat Fitzgerald and insisted he sit in. "At intermission, Serge got me in the alley," said Fitzgerald, "and said that Mel was only filling in while the band was in town and Serge pleaded with me to join the band . . . I thought real hard about it during the next set, and at the next intermission told him thanks, but no." As it turned out, the club owner wanted Chaloff to use drummer Chief McElroy, a popular local musician. They were often joined by saxman Dave Karr and Scott on vocals. Lou Levy was working across the street with trumpeter Conte Candoli, and the two groups would visit back and forth during breaks.

When that gig came to a close, Chaloff stayed in Minneapolis, hanging out with Dell Scott. Percy Hughes recalled Chaloff at the Minneapolis Flame: "Serge . . . was always at the Flame. At that time, I was doubling clarinet, alto and bari sax, so how do I tell a guy you've admired, 'I don't want you blowing my bari.' His mouth, his teeth were just black; I didn't know what to do, so I'd let him sit in and blow with us. I'd never touch the horn the rest of the night. Finally the union called me and told me, don't let him play." McCaffery took Serge to the airport and his mother paid to fly him back to Boston, where he died in 1957.

The names of Young, Pettiford, Chaloff, and others frequently show up in the annals of jazz history. The Twin Cities produced countless others with high-quality talent who are not immortalized in print but who are known to friends, colleagues, and professionals around the jazz world. The Twin Cities scene continues to add richness and quality in all styles—including Dixieland, which had its start during the early days of jazz and never really disappeared.

8

Way Up North in Dixieland

"Please do not mention modern jazz while people are eating."
—*Sign at Doc Evans's club, which featured Dixie and traditional jazz exclusively*

As far back as the days of riverboat bands, on through Prohibition, and into the 1930s era of swing, musicians associated with Dixieland and traditional jazz had performed widely in the Twin Cities. For many young musicians who would go on to play in different styles, Dixieland music was the first jazz they heard. For others, it was a style with which they remained linked throughout their careers. Progressive-jazz pianist Mickey McClain, dominant on the local scene in the 1960s, remembers at the age of ten walking down Hennepin Avenue with his dad. "I heard this Dixieland coming from one of the open doorways," he said. "I wanted to stop, but Dad said I couldn't go in there." David Bastien takes it back even further, remembering "going to the Curtis Hotel for my fourth birthday just after my father [Biddy Bastien] was discharged from the army. The band was a Dixieland band with my uncle, Fritz Hughart, playing bass. He was mainly known as an orchestra player, but he did some Dixieland jobbing back then."

One of Dixieland's best-known players, both locally and around the United States, was Paul "Doc" Evans, a multi-talented musician and music leader. Doc's son Allen understated it when he said, "A lot of people were interested in my father's music." A store in London, for instance, features an entire section of his music. In October 1958, the *Minneapolis Tribune* noted, "For six summers, Doc Evans's Dixieland band has drawn fans by the thousands to Walker Art Center's courtyard, sparking a resurgence of interest in New Orleans jazz."

Paul Evans, born in Spring Valley, Minnesota, in 1907, was surrounded by music, especially in the classical vein. He developed an insatiable appetite for listening. Later, his friend Fritz Lawrence, who had a large record collection, got Paul hooked on jazz. Evans attended Carleton College, where he began playing piano, drums, and sax in the Collegians band, but he soon learned his real love was the cornet. By the end of the Roaring Twenties, he was a regular on the Twin Cities music scene.

From the time the New Orleans Rhythm Kings first played the Marigold Ballroom in 1925, Dixieland increased in popularity in the Twin Cities. The popular early pianist Nettie Sherman blended Dixieland, ragtime, and the pop tunes of the 1920s. Over the years, more traditional styles of jazz such as Dixieland and swing generally stayed downtown and in hotels and country clubs, while the pre-bebop modernists who played more experimental jazz hit the after-hours spots, especially on Minneapolis's Near Northside.

While chamber of commerce promotions might not have mentioned jazz as a cultural asset in the 1930s, Dixielander names Doc Evans and Harry Blons occasionally surfaced in the press. Dixieland was the de facto public face of jazz in Minnesota. Doc played at Nisswa's Bar Harbor near Brainerd in 1936 with the Don Magnus Band and also played sax with Norvy Mulligan's group. He was once described as a very lyrical player who didn't play loud.

Doc quickly joined the ranks of trumpeters Les Beigel, Ferrol Wilson, and El Herbert as an in-demand player. In 1939, after Wilson (who was compared to Bix Beiderbecke) decided to hang it up and become a fisherman in Florida, Doc joined clarinetist-saxman Harry Yablonski (later Harry Blons), Eddie Tolck on drums and vibes, and Don Thompson on trombone. Red Dougherty put the band together for the opening of Herman Mitch's new nightspot in Mendota, just across the Mississippi from St. Paul. When the authorities went after the former speakeasy and gangster hangout, Mitch threw out the gambling tables and put in a stage. Mitch's thrived until World War II, when gasoline rationing kept people from driving out to the remote location.

Radio personality Leigh Kamman set up broadcasts from Mitch's with Sev Widman in the early 1940s. On the program *Studio Party Wham,* audience members answered quiz questions for free dinners, and Dougherty's band provided the music. "I suppose we were the forerunners of Dick Clark," said Kamman. After the radio duo split up, Kamman continued the program as *Matinee Wham* on the air at 4 PM Sundays.

Nationally known pianists Bob Zurke and Joe Sullivan played at Mitch's—Sullivan for a nearly eight-week run. Before his engagement, Sullivan insisted to Mitch, "I never drink on the job," but he fell off the bandstand the first night. Sullivan once played "Tea for Two" for a full hour, presumably not on the air. Drummer Eddie Tolck confirmed that "you couldn't beat him as a piano player, but when he drank, it sounded like he had boxing gloves on." Bob Zurke was just the opposite—he drank a lot, and it didn't seem to affect his playing.

Nationally, the forties saw what some called a New Orleans jazz revival, although others questioned whether this early jazz had ever really waned in popularity. In the Twin Cities, to be sure, the traditional sounds never went out of vogue. The spark of New Orleans jazz deposited here by the riverboat musicians and rekindled by the New Orleans Rhythm Kings during their 1925 tenure at the Marigold had been carefully tended and protected through the big band innovations of the Swing Era.

After World War II, Doc Evans, Harry Blons, and company fanned the Dixieland spark into flames when they realized they could both play in their style *and* please the public. "People wanted to hear pop tunes, but a band like this could make a Dixieland tune out of a pop tune," said Blons. Drummer Warren Thewis, who joined the band when Tolck left, was a good mechanic who constructed his own house in St. Paul. "Thewis could make a Dixieland band swing," said Dick Pendleton. "He seemed to have a sense of knowing just what you wanted in your choruses. He made you play better and had impeccable time." Pianist Butch Thompson said the group's players tried to sound like the old New Orleans musicians: "I used to get mad when people used the word *Dixieland,* but I'm not as upset about it as I used to be. I don't really know what it is; it does have a connotation of commercialism. I think the labels can be very misleading; the music is the thing. If it sounds good, if it's something that works, what's the difference what you call it?"

The Dixieland jazz session was held at the Prom Ballroom in 1960.

Doc Evans was more opinionated about changing trends in jazz. Commenting on the rise of swing music in the thirties, he noted: "Swing was a fancy dressing up, but also a dilution of jazz . . . Collective improvisation a la New Orleans and its immediate offshoots meant that each player tried to play what would best aid the overall ensemble. Teamwork was the essence of this type of playing, and it made for the best type of jazz. In the thirties, this sort of playing tended to disappear . . . It was replaced by virtuoso performances, every man for himself." Labeling newer styles "shallow, faddish, without emotional content," he added, "I've got an idea the American audience would rather hear Dixieland than any other kind of music—if it had the chance." Evans eschewed modernists like Miles Davis, who played a concert at the Tyrone Guthrie Theater for turning his back on audiences and ignoring fans, behavior Evans called hogwash. (He said he was in the phone book and would welcome the chance to chat with anyone who called.)

Evans played on Hennepin Avenue at the Roaring Twenties, a club trying to buck the Avenue's strip joint image by booking top instrumentalists. But as Butch Thompson pointed out, Doc Evans "was probably never more in his element than during his seven-year summer concert series at the Walker Art Center in Minneapolis, where he could bring in guests and showcase the music's grand history . . . Those events were worthy of the legendary status they eventually acquired."

Throughout his long career, Doc Evans played widely and continuously. He died January 10, 1977, after a meeting of the Musicians Local 73 board of directors. Guitarist Reuben Ristrom recalled, "It was a cold day, and Doc, who had some asthma issues, should have stayed home, but it was the first meeting after he and I had both been elected to the board. Doc's sense of duty overrode his common sense." Doc was inducted into the Minnesota Music Hall of Fame in 1989.

Doc's son Allen helped Jim Pilgrim get the annual Doc Evans Jazz Festival off the ground in Albert Lea, Minnesota: "I am still amazed at his loyal following. I continue to hear from his fans who . . . write to share their memories of meeting him, talk of first dates at his performance, or even the rush of nostalgia they get from just hearing one of his recordings again." Cornetist Jim Torok has been a Doc Evans stand-in at festivals and concerts: "Doc resurrected a huge repertoire of traditional tunes—

all sorts of classics—tunes they didn't play in his time, tunes they don't play now."

One of Doc Evans's frequent partners on the bandstand was Harry Blons, his name shortened from its original Yablonski (aka E. Blonski). Blons played at many of the well-known clubs and night spots, including the Criterion at University and Grotto in St. Paul, where he held forth with a quartet made up of Larry Wilson, Jerry Mayeron, and Eddie Tolck. The B&R Club at Dale and Selby in St. Paul, owned by Sugar Viner and Al Skibble, featured Blons with pianist Tommy McGovern and any number of players who stopped by to sit in. At the Bull Pen in Hopkins and Hennepin Avenue's Casablanca (later the Gay '90s), owned for a time by Herman Mitch, former Krupa trombonist Babe Wagner joined Blons, along with Tolck, Doc Evans, and Biddy Bastien. (Hal Runyon replaced Wagner when he decided to return to New Ulm and start an old-time band.) Nearby, Williams Bar opened with Dixieland music in 1953. Years later, when it moved up the street to Ninth and Hennepin, it dropped live music. Blons's house band opened the Blue Ox on Third Avenue in downtown Minneapolis and remained for several years. Reuben Ristrom came a bit later with Dick Bortolussi on drums. Around the same time, the Hall Brothers were playing Dixieland at Brady's. Drummer Bill Schneider, whose father played the first jazz young Bill heard in the early twenties, noted that most of the commercial arrangements coming out at that time were Dixieland tunes and said that when he went through his dad's library, he "must have found fifty tunes that we were playing with Harry Blons and Doc Evans at that time. They played a lot of ballrooms and pavilions . . . it was all danceable music."

Blons and Evans clashed at times over their approach to playing and their rapport with audience members. Bob Greunenfelder said Blons "would play any request the people wanted. Doc wouldn't. When a lady on the dance floor asked for 'Josephine,' he said to her, 'We don't play that kind of junk.'"

One of the top horn men of the day was Jerry Mullaney. Jerry "had a tremendous sound on the trombone," said Tolck. "He goes back into the big bands, Red Nichols's group and Will Osborne. He and Gene Bird, another good trombone player, grew up in Anoka. Doc van Deusen was one of the best. We had the old Mendota Buzzards down at the Emporium of

Paul "Doc" Evans was a strict traditionalist who didn't compromise his taste and musical values to follow trends.

Trombonist Jerry Mullaney (right, shown here with Kenny Ripple) was considered one of the tops on his instrument, but he had these observations about playing with the greats: "Typically, you'd get a chance to sit in with Lester Young and he'd literally blow you off the stand. In fifteen minutes you had your horn packed up and you'd be sitting there knowing he'd completely outshone you. So, you made up your mind that next time you sat in with him you'd hold your own. And you did. Today there's no such thing as that, where the young fellas can sit in."

Jazz before the guy closed it up. We had Red Wolfe's tribute down there. That was the last Dixieland that was played in the place."

Ervin "Red" Wolfe wasn't strictly a Dixieland trumpeter, but he played the music frequently. Born in Sauk Centre, Minnesota, he moved to Minneapolis at thirteen, attended Roosevelt High, and started playing professionally at seventeen. He hung out at Swing City in St. Paul and got some valuable coaching from Oscar and Ira Pettiford. He was a navy bugler during World War II and worked for the *Minneapolis Star* and *Tribune* newspapers when he returned. Wolfe started the Echoes of Ellington band in the early 1970s with Percy Hughes and Dick Norling and retired early, in 1978, to devote his life to music and education. He helped form the Port of Dixie Band in 1976 that played for more than a hundred thousand students. He died in 1991, the year he was inducted into the Minnesota Music Hall of Fame. His signature sign off to his audience was, "Keep Breathin' and Keep Swingin'!"

Wolfe played at a Dixie funeral for Twin Cities legend Norvy Mulligan, who died in 1985 at eighty-one after a long career in music and as a broadcaster at Anoka's KTWN. Norvy had started out playing hotels and country clubs in the 1930s and formed a booking agency with Gordy Bowen. They had an office over Crane's Bookstore near the university campus and once booked the Sportsmen's Show in Minneapolis at which a marksman accidentally killed the bass player. The next year clarinetist Dick Pendleton put a fake arrow on his head following an archery exhibition, resulting in the band being fired.

Dick Pendleton was another of the many Twin Cities jazz musicians who could have gone "big time" but opted to stay close to home. He was a fixture in Doc Evans's bands of the fifties and early sixties. He played full time and nixed opportunities to go on the road with Glenn Miller, Benny Goodman, and Ray McKinley. Pendleton died in 1999.

The Hall Brothers group and their close colleagues formed the nucleus of a traditional jazz scene in the Twin Cities that was unrivaled outside New Orleans. The original Hall Brothers band included Stan Hall on piano, Russ Hall on trombone, Charlie DeVore on cornet, Bill Evans, a trombonist who learned to play string bass, Dave Jackson on drums, and Dick Ramberg on clarinet. DeVore recalled, "I was very fortunate to have a lot of aspirations and dreams come true and meet those marvelous players."

One of Red Wolfe's later endeavors was the Port of Dixie Band. From top: Dick Norling, Al Closmore, Wolfe, Don Milleon, Dick Pendleton, Jerry Mullaney.

Record collector Kenny Hansen documented the Hall Brothers' evolution on tape, at rehearsals, and then gigs (tapes that now repose with collector-historian Kent Hazen). In the earliest years, the Hall Brothers emulated Dick Ramberg's Mississippi Counts, and the groups sometimes swapped players.

DeVore and Stan Hall met in 1958 when Stan would walk by Jim McDonald's Dixieland Record Heaven on his way home from Roosevelt

Red Wolfe led the Port of Dixie Band at the Gay '90s in 1952–53, moved to the Flame at Fourteenth and Nicollet, and recorded with an experimental eleven-piece group whose work was never released.

High School. The record store was sandwiched between a radio repair shop and the Chatterbox 3.2 saloon. McDonald had been a vaudeville drummer and did blurbs about visiting musicians for the local papers. "If it wasn't for McDonald, there wouldn't be a Hall Brothers," Butch Thompson said years later. McDonald "loved to play records, then argue about them. He would sit at the end of the bar [at the Emporium of Jazz] with a couple crates of records."

Stan Hall worked at Jinks Brady's Garage at 219 Oak Street near the university. The musicians turned it into a rehearsal hall, and Hall let people know when they were playing. Listeners came to party, but they never let it get out of hand. "We thought it was a good spot," said Hall. "We'd move cars so there was room and yank cushions out of them so people could sit. Our bouncer would intimidate folks into putting tips in [the] jar. We got eight hundred dollars once."

The Hall Brothers group started getting fraternity house gigs. Faculty members showed up, and the band played until 6 AM once a month.

At the same time the Hall Brothers traveled near and far, often just for gas money, from the Mound Casino on Lake Minnetonka and 'Nando's Hideaway near Ninety-eighth and Cedar to the East Grand Forks Officers' Club. Doc Evans told the young band that if they'd join the union, he'd hire them at his Rampart Street Club in Mendota. Doc eventually bailed out of the club, but clarinetist Loren Helberg took it over from co-owner Dave O'Dell. The club finally closed in December 1961.

It was in 1962 at Coffman Union on the university campus that Butch Thompson first met the Hall Brothers. Thompson was a freshman playing during their intermission and looking for someone to play for a twist dance contest. "I didn't know where they were coming from," said Thompson, so he didn't ask them to play. Thompson learned soon enough. He joined the band later that year when Ramberg moved to Doc Evans's group. Wisconsin drummer Doggie Berg also joined, replacing Jackson. Mike Polad succeeded Ron Strang on banjo and later switched to soprano sax. Polad and Thompson both played piano and clarinet.

DeVore first met Doggie Berg in an unusual setting—the back of a police paddy wagon in New Orleans. Both happened to be in the Crescent City in 1957 jamming with some local musicians who were arrested under an obscure ordinance that prohibited blacks and whites from socializing in that manner. A judge dismissed the charges, and several years later, back in Minneapolis, Doggie joined DeVore in the new Hall Brothers New Orleans Jazz Band. DeVore said when he met Butch Thompson, he played piano and clarinet like Brubeck and Goodman respectively and drove an old Nash-Kelvinator sporting a psychedelic paint job. When the band traveled to New Orleans in 1962, Thompson and the others got hooked on traditional New Orleans jazz after soaking it up at Preservation Hall.

Mendota's Emporium of Jazz, which the Hall Brothers band owned and operated with the help of some friendly investors, remained a bastion of traditional jazz from its opening on March 25, 1966, until it closed in 1991. Recalling the decision to open the club, DeVore said the Hall Brothers had wrapped up a gig at the Hopkins House, and they "went back to John Remarcic's place, and he and Stan drew up the ideas for taking over the old Rampart Street Club. Doc Evans had finished there in '61, and it had been lying dormant as more or less a little neighborhood 3.2 joint. They had at least half of it boarded up, so we leased the space. That's how the Emporium got its start." DeVore said, "Doggie Berg is the

On July 23, 1987, musicians and colleagues gathered to give Harry Blons a real New Orleans send-off.

guy that came up with the name of the club. Everywhere we'd play he'd say, 'Welcome to the Hopkins House . . . this is the Hopkins House Emporium of Jazz . . . ' or 'this is the Peacock Tavern House Emporium of Jazz.' He used that for everything, so that's what we called our place—'The Hall Brothers Emporium of Jazz.'"

The players felt they created their own ongoing jazz festival at the club, since it brought in legendary and historically significant traditional jazz veterans and touring revival bands from around the world. Stan Hall commented, "At the Emporium of Jazz for all those years, we played good jazz music every day." Thompson added, "It created a very unique atmosphere out there, something you wouldn't find any place else in town."

Reflecting back on the long run for Dixieland music in the Twin Cities, Butch Thompson noted, "Labels can be very misleading." But love it or hate it, Dixieland music elicits strong comments from local musicians of

Every year, the city of Albert Lea hosts the Doc Evans Jazz Festival. Here, the Bourbon Street Boys play for the seventh annual event, held in 2006.

all stripes. Harry Blons said that Dixieland "lets the musician express his moods . . . it's been recognized as a true American art form. It's been my first love for years." Doc Evans, who called it "hot jazz" and "historical," maintained that "people seem to have the feeling jazz is not quite respectable. They keep trying to bring it into a classical vein, trying to make it intellectual rather than emotional. Dixieland is emotional music." Musician Reuben Ristrom said, "you don't have to have a sophisticated knowledge of music for Dixie; other jazz you do." In the same vein, Bob Davis claimed, "Modern jazz deals in a higher technical understanding of music . . . Dixieland is a pure sound." Herb Pilhofer's assessment of Dixieland's place in jazz may just hit the mark: "The evolution from Dixieland to modern was natural. Each new group of musicians tries to establish a new style. Swing was an excess of Dixieland, and bebop was an excessive reaction to swing. Now we've got modern. Someday we will be considered traditionalists too."

9

From Swing to Bebop and Beyond

> "Jazz went from the classics to ragtime to Dixieland to swing to bebop to cool jazz, but it's always jazz. You can put a new dress on her, a new hat, but no matter what kind of clothes you put on her, she's the same old broad."
> —LIONEL HAMPTON, *musician*

While Dixieland held sway in some circles, other jazz filtered into the Twin Cities beginning in the 1930s. Traveling bands, small groups, radio, and records first introduced Twin Cities listeners to "swing"—danceable music performed by big bands like Benny Goodman's and Count Basie's. A few years later, they could hear what came to be known as bebop—more frenetic, complex music with extended virtuosic solos. From the late forties and into the fifties and sixties, more modern strains known variously as progressive, cool, avant-garde, and free jazz made their appearance.

One major Twin Cities musical event of the 1940s was the kickoff appearance of the very popular Glenn Miller Orchestra at the opening of Prom Ballroom in St. Paul on University. On a night in 1941, some six thousand revelers met at the Prom, which featured nearly a quarter-acre maple dance floor ringed by tables and booths where dancers could rest and socialize. A short time later, the Tommy Dorsey band booked there, prompting *DownBeat* to report, "Musicians were laying off in droves to attend the dance." Like the Marigold, its downtown Minneapolis counterpart, the Prom remained a popular gathering place where dancers could

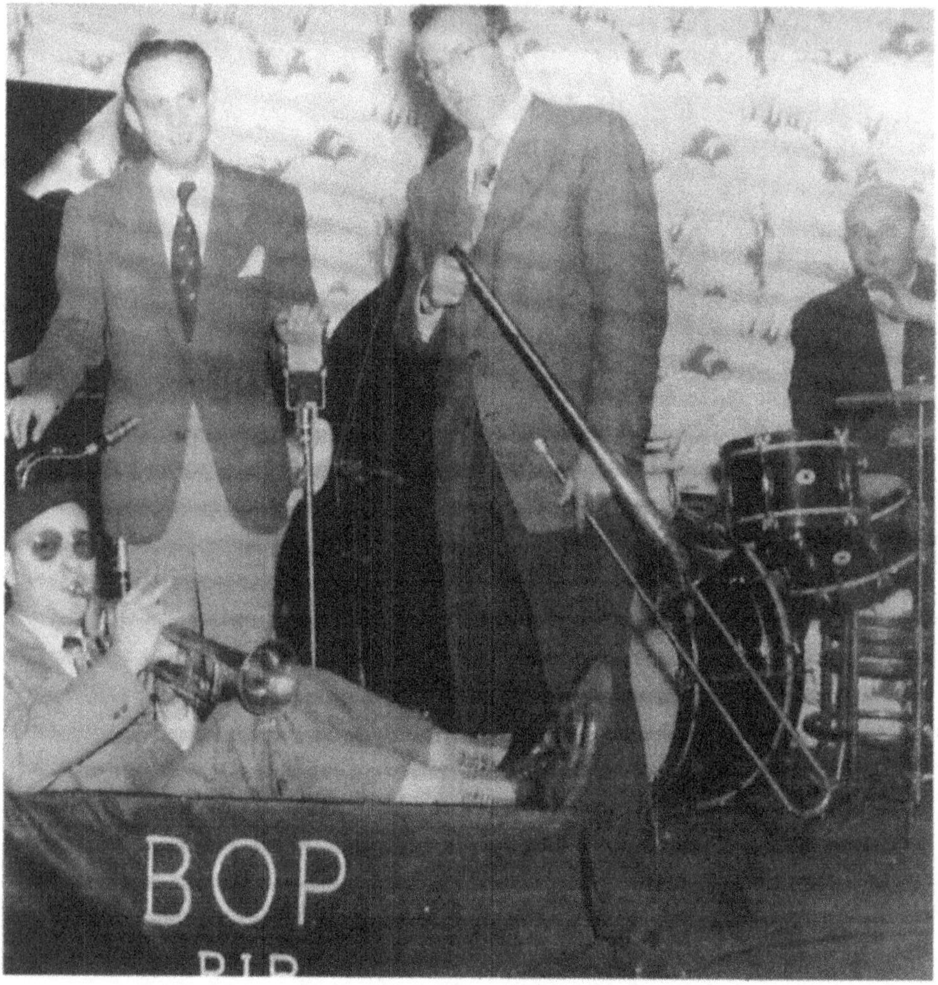

Bob Greunenfelder parodies a bebop trumpeter in a coffin at Mitch's in Mendota, symbolizing what he, Harry Blons, Hal Runyon, and Eddie Tolck hope is the demise of the new music emanating from New York's Fifty-second Street.

hear swing bands including Tommy and Jimmy Dorsey—as well as Count Basie, Stan Kenton, Buddy Rich, and many others before it met with the wrecker's ball in 1987.

The music rivalry between swing, Dixieland, and bebop that spread out from New York's lively Fifty-second Street scene did not help jazz music generally. Dave Karr, commenting on bebop saxophonist-composer

Mr. Smooth—Irv Williams—began playing in the Twin Cities with the Wold Chamberlin Navy Band in the 1940s. More than six decades later, he was still drawing crowds of local jazz fans.

Charlie Parker, noted, "A lot of people hated Bird when he started to play. Louis Armstrong did a very bad thing by dissing bebop. He called it 'Bop-Slop,' and immediately the camps sprang up."

One premier Twin Cities jazz musician who launched his career in the 1940s with swing-style music was saxophonist Irv Williams. Later known as "Mr. Smooth," a moniker bestowed by Bob Protzman in the *St. Paul Pioneer Press,* Williams arrived in the Twin Cities via Cincinnati, Little Rock, and St. Louis. His blossoming career was interrupted by the military, but after three years, he found himself at Wold-Chamberlin Naval Air Station playing in the highly regarded black navy band: "I was recruited from Louisville, Kentucky. The band director heard me play and said, 'We're going to the Twin Cities.' I said, 'I'm not going up there,' and he said, 'Yeah, you're going.'"

In the Twin Cities, Irv Williams met Duffy Goodlow, Frank Lewis, and a band full of good musicians who could both read music and improvise. After his discharge in 1945, Williams found that racism and being new in town initially made it hard for him to find work. When the Calhoun Beach Club's ballroom opened, he got his break and joined Stu Anderson on bass, Bob Dean on alto, and Bill West on trumpet as the nucleus of the

Irv Williams and pianist Peter Schimke in the studio recording one of their several CD projects in recent years.

club band. Over the decades, Williams worked virtually every club, hotel, and restaurant in the Twin Cities area.

Williams's friend Rufus Webster said, "You get to know a player's strengths and talents when you share a bandstand with them, learn things that elude the average listener. And *all* of Irv Williams's contemporaries, going back to the forties, have had the highest regard for his playing. He could have been just as prominent as any tenor player in the nation had he chosen that route. He's got tone and imagination. He's got a *great* ear. He's very selective in the notes that he plays. He plays correctly, and pleasingly." While Lester Young and Coleman Hawkins were early influences, Williams said that Stan Getz, his "all-time favorite, covers all the bases and does it well. Stan Getz is the epitome of a sax player."

Over his career Williams occasionally took a road gig. He got Ira Pettiford and Bob Crea to join him on the George Hudson band in the early fifties, playing the Apollo Theater, backing Ella Fitzgerald and Dinah Washington, and jamming with his friend Clark Terry. He had a chance to play with Basie at Freddy's in downtown Minneapolis: "Somebody had just left his reed section. I thought about it for a while, then didn't even show up." Williams explained, "The money wasn't right, and I was doing really well here in town."

Williams received a Lifetime Achievement award as a Jazz Master and Minnesota's governor proclaimed Irv Williams Day in 1984. He is an inductee into the Minnesota Jazz Hall of Fame. Now in his nineties, Williams said he "gave up quite a bit to live these few extra years . . . The doctors were talking about things that would have made me unable to play. I just want to be able to play." Now, he says, after seventy-five years of playing he "finally knows what it's about." In 2007, he recorded the CD *Finality,* which he insisted was his last, but he says that he still wants to record with two cellos "because of the timbre."

The Bastien family produced several players with significant musical accomplishments. Like the Pettiford and Peterson families, it was anchored by fine bassists. Vince Bastien was known for his work on WCCO as well as for playing on the local club scene. His brother Biddy went on to play bass with Gene Krupa's band in the late thirties and early forties. Biddy had a national reputation, and Vince was proud to read "in *DownBeat* and *Metronome* that Biddy was one of the top-ranked bass players." Another

Minneapolis bassist Biddy Bastien was in the Gene Krupa band at the time singer Anita O'Day and trumpeter "Sweets" Edison also shared the spotlight.

Bastien brother, tenor man Tony, went with Sonny Dunham, while Billy Bastien joined Claude Thornhill. While Vince hesitated to call the force that brought them all such good musical fortune a *mystique,* he said that the siblings "had a tremendous amount of pride and love," particularly from their parents.

An important player who successfully negotiated jazz genres that diverged in the last half of the twentieth century is reed virtuoso Dave Karr. With a career spanning more than fifty years, he ranks on most people's lists of top players, and to know his career of fifty-plus years is to know a significant chapter of local jazz history. Born in Canada in 1930, Karr spent some early years in England, where his father, a protégé of Rudy Wiedoeft, played saxophone for the BBC. When World War II erupted, Karr's uncle, Twin Cities businessman Benny Haskell, helped his family return to the United States, and Dave finished school in Queens, New York. He took piano lessons, but the saxophone intrigued him. Dave recalled, "Sunnyside, Queens, was quite a nice little musical community [of] six-story apartment buildings where . . . you'd hear guys playing bassoons and flutes and saxophones. One day in 1944, Dad left his saxophone out on the couch . . . and I said, 'Can I blow it while you're gone?' I knew how to not break the reed and everything, so he said, 'Sure, go ahead, have a ball with it.'" He did.

In 1949, Karr joined the musicians' union and played his first professional job in the Catskills. Back in New York City, he auditioned for the Sonny Dunham band and hit the road. He studied with Lee Konitz, who turned him on to Lester Young. Konitz told him to "learn Young's solos. Learn to sing them first. When you practice, use a metronome and practice with a strong sound and at a slow tempo, make the time with your fingers." Lee, Karr said, "didn't like Bird's mechanical vibrato [because it] . . . separated the swing and bop players from the cool players." An early influence on Karr was Charlie Ventura, whose solos Karr would memorize verbatim. Ventura got such a kick out of young Karr playing his solos that he would have Karr play for him on the stand in New York.

Karr's last road band was with Boyd Raeburn, and then the army intervened for three years. In 1954 Karr went to the Manhattan School of Music on the GI Bill: "Herbie Mann, Sam Most, John Williams [were there]. Naturally we were not going to take saxophone lessons. We were going to take advantage and take flute lessons with Harold Bennett. When there was a session, we would all blow flute. I kind of credit this with the beginning of the jazz flute . . . Herbie had it all planned out. He said, 'I'm going to be a famous jazz flute player. I'm not going to play the tenor anymore.' He wasn't my favorite player, but I do admire the way he pulled it off."

Karr soon moved to Minneapolis, attended the University of Minnesota, met Dede, his wife-to-be, and started playing with Dave Frishberg: "I loved playing with him. We had a little quartet we put together with Shelly Goldfus and Ted Hughart." At that time "Jim Hughart was just a young kid playing drums. Bob Kunin was one of the first guys I ran into in Minneapolis. He was very knowledgeable about jazz. He could voice nice changes on the piano, and he was a tenor player in the Al Cohn mold.

Saxophone colossus: Twin Cities reed giants Gary Berg, Dave Karr, Bob Crea, and Bob Kunin share the stage in 1958.

Very thoughtful, never missed a change." Frishberg was equally complimentary of his friend, saying Karr "was the best danged saxophone player I ever played with."

Also playing around the Twin Cities then was Serge Chaloff with Skip Christman, Jim Trost, and drummer Mel Leifman. Conte Candoli and Lou Levy were in town. Levy, who (like Chaloff) had recently left the Woody Herman band, played with trumpeter Don Specht at Coffman Union. The Hoop-D-Doo was going strong at Fifteenth and Nicollet—Bob Crea played in the house band with Bob Davis and Bill Blakkestad. Ray Komischke had a band at Duffy's at Twenty-sixth Street and Twenty-sixth Avenue South. Herb Pilhofer had arrived in '54 from Germany. During this period, Karr said, drug use was fairly common among musicians in the Twin Cities. He himself was "always a happy cat and evaded the heroin thing, but a lot of my friends were into it."

By the 1950s, Dave Karr was one of the most in-demand reed men around and a jazz force to be reckoned with. At left, drummer George Avaloz.

Karr got a good break when he got "the call" to go on the road with Bob Davis because Bob Crea wasn't available. While playing at the Blue Note in Chicago with the group, Karr did some commercial recording with Ramsey Lewis and recorded "Jazz in Orbit" with the Bob Davis Quartet. The players included Bill Blakkestad on drums, Bob Davis on piano, and John Frigo on bass and violin. Davis had done another recording, "Jazz from the North Coast," with Crea, Blakkestad, and bassist Stu Anderson.

Karr became an in-demand player for commercial jingles after a 1969 recording at Herb Pilhofer's pioneering Sound 80 studio. Karr recalled a night at Herb Klein's bar on Second Avenue North: "Advertising guys came in and asked Herb [Pilhofer] to play a few commercial spots. It turned out they paid him two hundred dollars for each spot. Pilhofer said,

Herb Pilhofer arrived in the Twin Cities from Germany in 1954 and immediately took up with the top players on the local scene. His trio of the middle fifties included guitarist Dale Olinger and Stu Anderson on bass.

'This is it for me. I'm not looking back.' In Minneapolis at that time there were one-hundred-plus ad agencies and lots of corporate headquarters. Herb had a good business head. He originally recorded at Kay Bank Studios at Twenty-sixth and Nicollet, which is still a recording studio called Creation Audio under the direction of owner Steve Wiese."

Karr paid his dues with a stint on the Jules Herman band and tried his hand at instrument repair but soon joined drummer Russ Moore at the new Duffy's bar on Twenty-sixth and Twenty-sixth, with Bob Jenkins on trombone, Jim Trost on piano, Jim Hughart on bass, and Bob Kunin or Gary Berg on baritone sax. He remembers an exciting time "when they brought Duke Ellington in for nine days, and we played intermissions and hung out with the band."

When the Tyrone Guthrie Theater opened in 1963, Karr was on the staff band for eight seasons. Because he was making only $168 a week at the Guthrie, he quit and opened his own business writing music for radio and TV commercials and arranging for vocalists: "My last six-night-a-week job was at the Thunderbird in 1970 with Carole Martin, George Avaloz, and Mickey McClain. I had five kids now, and I was making a good living with the commercial and jingle thing. Jazz took a back seat even though jazz never took a back seat in my mind and heart. I listened and practiced as much as I could, and I would go sit in and play as much as I could."

It was the end of the fifties when Karr realized he wouldn't be going back to the New York scene: "I felt I had lost that hard edge: 'Give *me* the job, man.' And when I got the writing bug, I realized I liked that, and I'm playing music and making money, and my kids are healthy. When guys you know and respect think you're playing good, that's making it. Plus the music that I like doesn't have mass appeal. I always thought that playing and writing any kind of music was better than not playing at all."

Karr continued writing, arranging, and performing, finally abandoning all but playing in the new century. In 2007, he was awarded a $25,000 McKnight Fellowship for excellence in instrumental performance. Herb Pilhofer sums up a musicians' consensus view of Karr's abilities: "Dave has this knack to play the right thing; a gift to play for the moment." Pilhofer recalled sitting in the audience at the Guthrie when Karr played solo clarinet for the play *Thieves' Carnival*. A woman leaned over and said, "You know, for an actor, the guy plays pretty good clarinet."

10
The Clubs

"Music can be made anywhere, is invisible, and does not smell."
—W. H. Auden

Finding live jazz in the Twin Cities today requires some planning. Gone are the days when nightspots clustered in the two downtowns or in neighborhoods like the Near Northside. The Dakota Jazz Club in Minneapolis and the Artists' Quarter in St. Paul have regular offerings, but what else? Rossi's, Jazzmines, the Turf Club's Clown Lounge, and the Times are past tense. Occasional venues include the Riverview Cafe, the West Bank School of Music, O'Gara's Garage, Famous Dave's, and the Capri and Old Log theaters. There are others, to be sure, but most spots feature jazz interspersed with an eclectic mix of R&B, pop, rock, and hip-hop, sometimes to the confusion of would-be patrons who are not sure what to expect or who arrive expecting jazz and get something else. But there was a time when listeners knew what they wanted and where to get it, and they returned again and again to hear first-rate talent at well-known local clubs and large venues.

For a long time, the tiny community of Mendota on the river bluff was a focal point for jazz. Jax Lucas, a professor and a stringer for *DownBeat* magazine, once dubbed Mitch's "the Nick's of the Midwest," after the famous Dixieland house in Greenwich Village. Herman Mitch first opened the club in 1939, having previously run the Silver Stripe at Dale and Selby in St. Paul. Pianist Red Dougherty served as mayor of the hamlet in the

Red Dougherty, here with bassist Bernie Sundermeyer, served as mayor of Mendota and ran the successful Parker House supper club.

late thirties and early forties. He also owned the popular Parker House restaurant, an upscale eatery that became Axel's River Grille.

In 1949 Leigh Kamman's *Dixieland Caravan* emanated from the re-opened Mitch's, run by Herman's son, Bob. The program featured the Mendota Buzzards, Harry Blons's band with Eddie Tolck on drums and vibes. Tolck said, "Those were fun days. Anybody that meant anything who was in town would be there. Bob Eberle, [Jack] Teagarden, [Lawrence] Welk's sidemen. The program was somewhat scripted but informal." Also in Blons's new band were several players from the first Mitch's, Hal Runyon, bassist Willie Sutton, and saxophonist Dick Pendleton. The newcomers included Lyle Smith, Russ Moore, and Warren Thewis, successively, on drums, Jerry Mayeron followed by Hod Russell on piano, and Bob Greunenfelder on trumpet. Shortly after, however, highway construction closed the club for good in October 1950.

Mendota had more than its per capita share of clubs over the years. There was Doc Evans's Rampart Street Club (1958–61), which had been the Bow and Arrow and later morphed to become a rock club, Ragin' Cajun. There was also the Colonial, Gay Paree, and the Hollywood. Listeners found the nearby River Road Club—known for its unruly clientele and the music of Cornbread Harris and Augie Garcia—by taking a shortcut through the Emporium's parking lot. Prior to the club's closing, several people misjudged the road and ended up in the river.

Another popular locale for listeners to find clubs, theaters, and strip joints offering music had been the Avenue in Minneapolis. Beginning during Prohibition, musicians played on Hennepin Avenue six or seven nights per week. A partial listing of downtown places to hear jazz included Augie's (424 Hennepin, earlier Lindy's and Crombie's), Bellanotte (600), Brady's (also near Sixth), Camel's Club (520), Casablanca (408—later the Gay '90s), Coconut Grove (above Brady's), Frolics (516, moved to Third Street in the fifties), Gallery, Jockey Club (507—previously Vic's, the Dome, Osterberg's), Moose Lodge, Orpheum Theatre, Palace Theater (424), Paradise (414½), Poodle, Red Feather, Roaring Twenties, Roberts Café, Saddle, Sleizer's, Spud's, Walker Art Center, and Williams.

For many years, Minneapolis's Near Northside was a most-happening locale for clubs. Operating at one time or another, some with longevity, were the Clef Club, Club DeLiza, Club Morocco (aka Kongo, King Kong), Cotton Club, Chicken Shack, Ebony Social Club, Elks Rest, Gin Mill, Harlem Breakfast Club (previously Musicians Rest, 141 Hyland Avenue North), El Grotto (later Howard's Steak House—in the fifties at 715 Olson Highway), the Hub, the Nest, Old Southern Barbecue (700 North Lyndale), Peggy's, Rhumboogie (128 Highland, previously the Maple Leaf), the Spot,

Mitch's in Mendota was the place to go for traditional and Dixie in the early forties.

and Wondervue. Herb's Bar, another popular club, opened downtown in 1946 at Third and Marquette, but in 1961 it moved to Second Avenue North to escape urban redevelopment. Herb Klein hosted top local jazz names including his house trio of Herb Pilhofer, Bob Pope on drums, and both Hughart bassists, Ted and Jim. Pianist Pat Moran, whom Geordie Hormel had brought to Irv Schechtman's White House in Golden Valley, was play-

Mitch's, at the intersection of Highway 55 and 100 (later 110), thrived in the early forties, closed during the war, reopened in 1949, and was demolished the following year to make way for highway construction.

ing at Herb's with Buddy DeFranco in 1965 when burglars using an acetylene torch caused a major fire in the bar that severely damaged Paul Warburton's bass.

Another Minneapolis spot near Seven Corners, now crossed by Interstate 35W, was South of the Border Bar, augmented by the Key Club in 1951. Always a place to find top local talent, the club welcomed such nationally known artists as Sonny Stitt, John Coltrane, and Miles Davis.

St. Paul also had its live-music clubs. It hosted the Dakota beginning in the 1980s before the club left Bandana Square for its posh digs on the Nicollet Mall. The city is still home to one of the Twin Cities' premier listening rooms, the Artists' Quarter, now in its second downtown location since leaving Twenty-sixth and Lake Street in Minneapolis. Drummer Kenny Horst, who runs the Artists' Quarter, quipped during the recent economic downturn, "The good thing about jazz is you don't notice the recession. It's never great, but the audience is steady." Horst also noted

Drummer and club owner Kenny Horst grew up in the same St. Paul neighborhood as George Avaloz.

changes in the jazz-club scene: "You used to get Bill Evans or Dizzy Gillespie for two weeks. Now, you're lucky if you can book someone for a couple of nights." Horst adds that musicians call him from New York and elsewhere offering to play for a percentage of the door: "In our day, we wanted a guarantee. Now, club owners want a guarantee. There are not a lot of people out there that can draw."

Jazz historian Kent Hazen says that Horst has had a keen sense for programming: "Kenny was very entrepreneurial in his ability to seek out a backer or talk some club owner into having a jazz quality. He was very persistent and has kept the public awareness of jazz at as high a level as it could be with little or no help." Horst now co-owns the Artists' Quarter along with musicians Billy and Ricky Peterson and Hod Boyen, plus Jerry Kennelly.

The Artists' Quarter has managed to bring in some big names in jazz as well as some familiar visitors who were once a part of the local jazz fabric.

Bob Rockwell cut his musical teeth in the Twin Cities and now makes his home in Copenhagen, Denmark.

One such artist is expatriate saxophonist Bob Rockwell. Shortly after beginning his jazz adventure as a teen listening to Gerry Mulligan, Dexter Gordon, Coltrane, and Sonny Rollins, Rockwell played with a group of his young peers at Minneapolis's Fireside Pizza at Sixty-sixth and Penn Avenue. He hooked up with Bloomington trumpeter-leader Dick Whitbeck's Blue Diamonds big band and hit the session scene as often as possible at the Padded Cell, McGoo's, Big Al's, and the Turtle Club, an after-hours joint in St. Paul. Rockwell recalled that Jimmy Hill "took me over to Central and introduced me to Bobby Lyle. Walter Thornton played piano there. Charlie Gator was at the Cassius and Buddy Davis at Big Al's. The older musicians mostly told me what not to do: Know the tunes, don't practice during other guys' solos." A stay in New York City helped hone Rockwell's reading and improvising skills. "Man, that was a hell of a trip," Rockwell said. "Why? I went to New York and I learned to play the blues."

In the seventies Rockwell helped found the jazz fusion group known as Natural Life, which blended the funky elements of rhythm and blues with the improvisation of jazz. Natural Life included guitarist Mike Elliott, bassist Billy Peterson, pianists Tommy O'Donnell and Bobby Peterson, and drummers Bill Berg, Eric Kamau Gravatt, Joey Piazza, and Paul Lagos at various times. Rockwell recorded "Jungleopolis," given a five-star rating by *DownBeat* in 1974, with pianist Art Resnick, Billy Peterson, and Paul Lagos. Before Rockwell moved to Denmark in 1983, he told Bob Protzman in a *DownBeat* interview that he wanted to remain in the Twin Cities: "I've been to the coasts and I don't care for the way you have to live." After nearly three decades in Europe, Kenny Horst said Rockwell appeared to be there for the duration: "He loves it."

One early local influence on Rockwell was tenor man Jim Marentic, another refugee of the strip joint wars. Marentic played at Herb's, a downtown night spot, in 1964. He joined in on a pirated recording in 1967 made at the university's Coffman Union with Mickey McClain, Kenny Horst, and Jay Goetting, an amazingly advanced avant-garde outing for the young players. Marentic took up bass, studied with Art Gold, and headed for Los Angeles in 1975 and then to the Big Apple. He also learned piano tuning. "I was intimidated because of the heavy players like Tom Harrell," said Marentic, who ended up being one of the heavy hitters himself, backing Anita O'Day and traveling to Hong Kong and Europe. He returned to the Twin Cities and continued writing as well as teaching and

Bassist Billy Peterson, part-owner of St. Paul's premier jazz club, the Artists' Quarter, was a founding member of Natural Life and has associated with such artists as Ben Sidran and Steve Miller.

playing tenor sax and bass, aided by grants from the National Endowment for the Arts and other organizations. McClain would eventually go to New York to play in the Catskills. Sax player Dave Karr said McClain would show up at sessions and put off some of the other players because "guys disliked his playing, mainly because they didn't understand what he was doing." Karr said that McClain "wasn't that 'out' of a player. Later, he became mainstream, and all of a sudden everybody likes Mickey more. I don't think he changed; I think the people kinda got used to it."

McClain said he realized he had come in for a good deal of "scurrilous criticism" but also got enough positive input to pursue his musical goals. He developed a meticulous and complex approach to harmony that he found went over the heads of many, especially horn players who played "by ear" but improvised wonderfully "in spite of their ignorance of harmony." But he was not arrogant in his approach. Universally liked, McClain went on to play with the Buddy Rich Band, Clark Terry, and Johnny Hartman, among others. In recent years, he has lived quietly in upstate Afton, New York.

Natural Life's Mike Elliott created quite a splash when he hit the Twin Cities scene in 1966, and he is fondly remembered by colleagues like drummer Joey Piazza, Gary Berg, pianist Tommy O'Donnell, and Rockwell. Elliott had grown up in Colorado, where he studied with Johnny Smith, and went on the road before joining Natural Life, which played at the Longhorn in Minneapolis. Elliott moved to Nashville in the early eighties and worked as a studio musician before his death in 2005.

Another young lion from Natural Life was pianist Bobby Peterson, a member of the well-known Peterson clan that enriched the Twin Cities scene. Bobby Peterson, like Bobby Lyle at almost the same time, became known as a "phenom" with exceptional technical skills and "big ears." Not only did Peterson join with the contemporary players of the sixties and seventies but he was in demand to play with Irv Williams, Dave Karr, and other veterans. He toured with the Buddy Rich Band when he was in his early twenties. In 2002, Bobby Peterson died on the bandstand at age fifty-two.

Many jazz followers consider the Peterson family a dominant force in Twin Cities music for decades. Willard "Willie" Peterson married Jeanne Arland in 1942. "We'd work the nice hotels, sometimes two pianos," recalled Jeanne. "Willie started at 'CCO in '51 and stayed 'til '60." The two

This publicity shot dates to 1942, the year Jeanne Arland married Willie Peterson and started a musical dynasty in the Twin Cities.

Peterson family portrait, c. 1975: front: Paul; middle: Linda, Patty, Jeanne; back: Rick, Billy

performed together until 1967 and had six children: Linda, Billy, Patty, Ricky, Jeffrey, and Paul. Willie was the first organist for the Minnesota Twins baseball team, and he died on opening day in 1969. Jeanne said, "They found someone to replace him for a few days, and then I did it for three years."

Jeanne Arland Peterson came from a musical family and began singing in a band with her brother at age fifteen. In 1938, someone at WCCO heard the talented youngster at the Coconut Grove, above Schinder's newsstand on Hennepin, and at Brady's Bar at Sixth and Hennepin. Jeanne's career was off and running. She teamed with Bob DeHaven on *Breakfast With Bob* at 8:45 weekdays on the Midwest's dominant radio station. "That was my second home," she said. "We got to be well acquainted with the singers and musicians and emcees. It was always fun to go down there." Jeanne was only the second woman—after Judy Garland—to be inducted into the Minnesota Music Hall of Fame. Jeanne cited a highlight of her career as a 1958 concert at the Met Stadium with Paul Whiteman conducting the Minneapolis Symphony. Twin Cities sax legend Frankie Roberts recalled playing society gigs with Willie and Jeanne Peterson and having "a little fun at the St. Paul Athletic Club with Jeanne on organ, with drums and horn, and sometimes Larry Malmberg on accordion."

Jeanne and Willie's oldest child, singer-songwriter Linda Peterson, performed internationally; her sister Patty is a jazz and R&B artist who has also worked as a talk show host on WCCO, KSJN, and KBEM.

Brother Billy Peterson began singing commercials at age nine, studied drums, and picked up both electric and acoustic basses in his early teens. After cofounding Natural Life in 1973, he played at the Longhorn Cafe, a popular jazz spot in the sixties and seventies run by the owners of Hennepin Avenue's Poodle. Billy recorded prolifically and played extended road tours with the Steve Miller Band, Leo Kottke, and others. With saxman Bob Rockwell, he once played the Blue Note in Milan, Italy. Billy calls the Artists' Quarter, which he co-owns, his home base when he's not on the road.

Brother Ricky Peterson, well known for his B-3 organ skills, has served as music director for artists like George Benson and David Sanborn. Youngest sibling Paul has stayed in the pop genre, backing Prince and Stevie Wonder and as bassist and music director for Donnie Osmond.

Another branch of the extended Peterson family tree produced more Twin Cities musicians. Patriarch Willie's brother had played violin and done a radio show with accordionist Myron Floren in Sioux Falls, South Dakota, before the family moved to Minneapolis. His daughter Carol is a vocalist. Son Russ Peterson became a pivotal player on the Twin Cities scene, a multi-instrumentalist who mostly plays sax. Sibling Tom Peterson went west years ago, as brother Russ put it, "to find fame and fortune. He paid the price. It's a hard way to do it. You go to every rehearsal, go with everyone who calls." This paid off since Tom subbed all the Los Angeles woodwind chairs and played television's *Tonight Show* for seventeen years. Russ went on the road for a while after the army but returned to the Twin Cities and, like many of his colleagues, paid his dues in "stage clubs" on the Avenue. Russ got into Dixieland with drummer Bob Gilbertson and joined with Reuben Ristrom, Jay Epstein, Keith Boyles, and Ron Seaman in various groups known as the Bourbon Street Boys, the Riverboat Ramblers, and Seaman's contemporary B-3 group, TC Jazz Cartel.

Bobby Lyle, another pianist with incredible chops, played widely in clubs while growing up in the Twin Cities. He occasionally returns to the Dakota. When the teenage Lyle began playing in Hennepin Avenue clubs, the musicians at Augie's had to get special permission not only from Bobby's family in South Minneapolis but from the "morals squad" of the Minneapolis Police Department. Pianist Herb Schoenbohm recalls teenager Lyle sitting in at the Valli Pizza in Dinkytown. Bobby soon became a familiar presence on the Hammond B-3 at Big Al's, the Blue Note, and Road Buddies' Ebony Lounge. Organist Billy Holloman, who likened his own "old style" to Bobby's and to jazz master Jimmy Smith's, said Bobby played "a thick, swirling, swinging blend of funk, gospel, R&B, and of course jazz." Lyle's later forays into a more pop-oriented music scene with Sly and the Family Stone, Al Jarreau, Anita Baker, and Bette Midler moved him toward fame as a "smooth jazz" artist, although he was fully capable of getting into a groove when called upon.

Lyle's early colleagues in Minneapolis included the Hubbard brothers, Gene and Jerry, on guitar and drums, respectively, along with drummer Bill Hobbs, saxman Dean Brewington (known early in his Twin Cities tenure as Norwood Dean), trumpeter Mel Carter, and Bobby's brother Ollie Lyle on bass. Bobby's musical partners offer him accolades. Perry Peoples said, "I first heard him in '57 at the Red Feather Club on University Avenue.

Bobby Lyle has accompanied and served as music director for many big-name artists, but he still occasionally returns to his old stomping grounds to perform.

Bobby was next door. I thought I was listening to Oscar Peterson." Another great Twin Cities keyboardist, Mickey McClain, said that when Wynton Kelly was playing at Herb's (with Paul Chambers and Jimmy Cobb), the sixteen-year-old Lyle walked in during a smoke break: "Bobby played, and Kelly looked up and exclaimed, 'Who the f*** is that?'" McClain also cited a gig at the Leamington Hotel with Trevor Koehler on baritone sax: "Bobby would come in where I was playing, and the audience would go nuts. He sounded like a combination of Rachmaninoff and Tatum."

Coffman Union on the University of Minnesota campus, while not literally a "club," functioned as a regular jazz venue for many years. It has been the site of a lot of good jazz, from the Oscar Pettiford–Dmitri Mitropoulos boogie-woogie escapade in 1941 to present-day performances in a downstairs spot known as the Whole. Coffman's heyday may have come in the 1960s, when Kent Hazen led the Jazz Workshop committee and wrote jazz reviews for the *Minnesota Daily* newspaper. Besides tapping local players like Bobby Lyle, Stan Haugesag, Dave Moscoe, Jerry Rusch, and Don Rustad, Hazen managed to fill the theater "to the rafters" with visiting firemen like Gene Krupa, Earl "Fatha" Hines, New Orleans clarinetist George Lewis, Pepper Adams, and, almost, Thelonious Monk. Monk was booked for an engagement at Davey Jones' Locker at the Downtowner Motel, but he was unwilling or unable to play one night. (Local pianist Dave Moscoe got the call to fill in, and he made the date with Charlie Rouse on tenor, bassist Larry Gales, and drummer Ben Riley.) Monk was also a no-show for the Coffman gig. Hazen recalled, "When my right-hand committee member and friend John Hollenhorst and I went to the Downtowner to bring him to the gig, Monk was fully involved in the behavior he had begun exhibiting over the weekend. He refused to do the gig, and nothing would persuade him to come with us. We had no alternative but to return to Coffman empty handed, where I had to tell the packed house that there would be no concert. It's a testament to 'Minnesota nice' that aside from a huge collective groan, there was no ugly reaction from this mass of humanity, vocal or otherwise."

Although some Twin Cities club owners and players say the local jazz scene today is among the strongest in the United States, the financial stability of jazz clubs ebbs and flows. After Lowell Pickett opened the Dakota Bar and Grill in 1985 with a policy of hiring local musicians, a persistent agent countered Pickett's claim that he couldn't afford to hire nationally known pianist McCoy Tyner. In this case the offer of a nice piano and good accommodations brought Tyner on board. Musician referrals led to more celebrity bookings with the likes of Carmen McRae, Freddie Hubbard, and Ahmad Jamal. In recent decades the Dakota experienced financial woes and then stabilized before facing eventual bankruptcy. Pickett sold memberships and regained some footing, but it was when Richard and Julie Erickson purchased an interest in the club and moved it to Minneapolis that things picked up again. The music bookings became a mix of jazz, pop, and R&B, which Horst characterized as "less jazz and much less local."

Clubs and restaurants affiliated with hotels, country clubs, ballrooms, auditoriums, and concert halls have also helped provide Twin Cities listeners with the jazz music they love and given musicians (usually) suitable podiums for expression. Among the hotels offering music were the St. Paul Hotel and its Gopher Grill; the Lowry Hotel's Terrace Café; the Commodore; the Radisson (beginning in 1909); the Nicollet's Minnesota Terrace; the Curtis; the Twin Cities Winter Jazz Festival at the Millennium Hotel; the St. Louis and Del Otero at Lake Minnetonka, where swingers danced until it burned down on July 4, 1945; the Sheraton Ritz's Golliwog Lounge, which featured singer Dick Mayes and pianists Jim Trost, Manfredo Fest, and Bobby Peterson; and another Ritz on Washington Avenue in the 1930s. Among the seedier establishments were the Andrews; the Seville near the Milwaukee Road Depot, and the New Brighton, where drummer Joe Kimball played his first gig in 1920. There was the Taft, the Rogers, and the Russell in the 1930s, and of course, Minneapolis's big Leamington Hotel, built in 1912 and demolished eighty years later. Some Twin Citians traveled to Duluth to hear Red Maddock, Bud Damon, and Nate Wexler at the Lennox Hotel. The Mar-Key sessions in the Hastings Hotel were well attended and often drew visiting firemen such as Rahsaan Roland Kirk and Thelonious Monk.

Local bands at Twin Cities hotels included Mickey McClain, George Avaloz, familiar faces like Jack Coan, and new faces such as baritone players Trevor Koehler and Les Rout, trumpeter Jerry Rusch, and tenor man Jules Goldberg. The tall, redheaded Koehler, originally from New Orleans, played a contemporary style, fronted a group in California, and played some dates with Gil Evans before his death in 1976. Coan and Rusch moved to California and met with considerable success. Rout taught history at the university after playing with Paul Winter's group.

The Tyrone Guthrie Theater, which opened in 1963 adjacent to the Walker Art Center in Minneapolis, was long a preeminent jazz concert venue. For eight years Herb Pilhofer led and wrote for a group there that included multi-reed man Dave Karr, drummer Russ Moore, bassist Ted Hughart, trumpeter Jack Coan, Paul Binstock on French horn, and Stan Haugesag on trombone. Haugesag praised Pilhofer's work: "The group was very tight because of Herb's insistence on rehearsing everything what seemed like a million times. We were very proud of our performances at places like the Walker Art Center jazz series and various colleges. Pilhofer did a great deal for Twin Cities jazz and recording."

The Guthrie hosted a parade of jazz all-stars in the 1960s that included Miles Davis, Charles Mingus, Bill Evans, and John Coltrane. Local bassist Maurice Turner recalled the Coltrane concert when the rhythm section of Ron Carter, Elvin Jones, and McCoy Tyner missed its plane. Turner, who got a last-minute call to play the 1964 concert, stopped by Biddy Bastien's to borrow his bass. "There was no rehearsal," said Turner. "[Trane and I] sat backstage and talked through the show. Later, this mild man turned into this giant. It was like Jekyll and Hyde." Dub Frazer, a Chicago pianist then living and working in Minneapolis, subbed for Tyner.

The Padded Cell, a 3.2 beer joint at Lake Street and Colfax Avenue that opened in 1953, was a favorite spot for jam sessions as well as name entertainment. Owner Paul Fink, a former correctional officer at San Quentin prison and San Francisco cop, charged ninety-nine-cent admission to hear the likes of Charlie Ventura, Buddy DeFranco, Kai Winding, Henry "Red" Allen, and locals Doc Evans, Harry Blons, and a young group out of Edina, the Dixieland Ramblers. In the sixties, Reuben Ristrom, Eddie Berger, Lee Pierson, "Tiny" Reichel, and Jan Jacobson formed the nucleus for the Sunday evening jams. "Tiny, like many others in those days, liked to have a few drinks and was always ready to give the bass to anyone who cared to sit in," said Ristrom, "much to the delight of the rest of the band—especially if the person wanting to sit in was someone else of higher musical stature than Tiny, which included most of the bass players around."

Many jazz greats would show up and sit in after they had played a concert in town. Gary Berg said Fink, who kept monkeys in cages until the health department nixed his menagerie, "had a woman in a bathing suit swinging on the beer sign outside. It was a hip place. He really tried hard to keep jazz in the place. He broke down a wall and expanded with a Charburger. He kept that portion of Lake Street going." Fink eventually returned to the West Coast as the folk music craze overtook jazz in the 1960s.

Over the years the Twin Cities has served as a "farm system" for the musical big leagues, sending many of its best players off in search of greener pastures. Some, like Jack Coan and Don Specht, found those emerald meadows in California. Both played in the award-winning Bruce Dybvig band when it won the *Look* magazine award in 1946 for best young band. Specht played trumpet and piano and arranged for bands around the Twin Cities before heading for Hollywood, and he even maintained a studio in London. The pair made up the core of some strong trumpet sections locally that included Richard Zemlin, Sammy Haverson, and Bill Cottrell. They played with Jerry Tressman, bass clarinet, Paul Katruud, piano, and Stu Anderson on bass. Two young fans, Dave Frishberg and Bob Oches, regularly showed up at Howard's Steak House in the 1950s with a wire recorder. (It is doubtful that any of those recordings have survived.) After Coan moved to California, he played with the Don Ellis band, with Bill Holman, and in the studios.

Young Dave Frishberg came out of St. Paul Central High School and began playing at the university with other up-and-coming professionals—Coan, Ted Hughart on bass, saxman Dave Karr, "best buddy" Dick Thompson, also a bassist from Macalester College, drummer Shelly Goldfus, Dave Kuain, Dick Zemlin, Norman Nelson, Ray Komischke, and Don Ellis. Frishberg only played piano. "It never entered my mind to sing," he said. After graduation, he played at the Key Club on Washington Avenue with Hensley Hall and Mel Leifman. Then off to New York he went, gaining fame as a songwriter-singer as well as a pianist. Frishberg lists Dave Karr among those who most influenced his career: "Karr is one of the most profound influences on my music—his excellence and musicality... He was the most proficient musician I had met at the time."

Don Ellis, a minister's son, used Minneapolis's Wesley Temple as a rehearsal hall for his early band activities while attending West High. For a time Ellis played trumpet with the Glenn Miller Orchestra under Ray McKinley, leaving in 1956. His experiments with unusual time signatures would become legend, a skill honed in his octet with Dave Karr,

Dave Frishberg, Russ Moore, Stan Haugesag, Ted Hughart, and Justin Fink. Karr recalled playing with a black flugelhorn player who also wrote named Hensley Hall: "We used to play a lot together on Saturday night jobs and jam sessions with Bill Boone, Eddie "the Mole" Bourne, Buddy Davis, and Bryce Robertson, a white guitar player raised by black people [who] was the 'downest' guitar player. There were a lot of after-hours houses where you could shoot craps, booze, hang out, and jam."

Drummer George Avaloz grew up on St. Paul's West Side Mexican American community. He left for Chicago at the urging of vocalist Billy Eckstine, with whom he sat in at Minneapolis's Key Club on Washington Avenue. The singer eventually hired him. Their relationship lasted ten years and greatly influenced Avaloz's own vocal style. He also spent time in the jazz mecca of New York City in the seventies, playing with Jackie McLean and Clifford Jordan before returning to his roots in the early eighties. He settled back in the Twin Cities, where he has played at numerous venues including the Dakota and the Artists' Quarter. Over the decades, nightclubs, swank hotel ballrooms, theaters, and seedy dives have come and gone—mostly gone. While the roster is not as broad and diverse as it once was, participants agree that the Twin Cities remains a bastion for jazz and its purveyors.

11

The Big Bands

"I liked every band I ever played in because each band was different, each band had a different concept, and each band leader was different . . . different personalities and musical tastes."

—Buddy Rich

As jazz moved from the speakeasy to the ballroom, the emergence of large ensembles of musicians playing smooth, rhythmic "swing" music fostered the term "Big Band Era." Most famously played by Benny Goodman's and Count Basie's bands, big band swing remained popular until the advent of faster-paced bebop in the early 1940s changed tastes again, especially among jazz insiders. The World War II draft also decimated some popular bands, plucking away such players as Biddy Bastien, Percy Hughes, Irv Williams, Ernie Charleston, and young broadcaster Leigh Kamman from the local scene. By the 1950s, television, the new electronic marvel—or evil—threatened to replace most live entertainment.

Big bands had formed the basis for early radio broadcasts from the Twin Cities' large hotels like the St. Paul, the Lowry, and the Radisson. Bill Schneider recalls, "In the thirties, jazz was becoming more accepted. The Coliseum at Lexington and University and the Boulevards of Paris had lots of big bands. The Plantation at Wildwood [on White Bear Lake] had one of [the] biggest pianos I'd ever seen, all hand carved and bullet holes around it. Pretty Boy Floyd, Dillinger, Machine Gun Kelly, that was their spot, and they didn't play nice." The Boulevard charged a dollar cover when the big bands were in town. Joe Jung's good big band played at the Lowry Hotel's Terrace Café. Throughout the thirties, big bands provided the most common music heard in public venues all over the country, from plush pavilions to the corrugated-metal buildings found in most rural communities that had more than a Main Street and a saloon.

Big bands, often consisting of ten or more players, provided a good source of work for musicians and often served as a player's ticket out of town if he was hoping to hit the big time. One of the first to make the great escape from the Twin Cities to a truly great big band was Lester Young, who jumped from the El Patio to the Count Basie band. Oscar Pettiford's runs with Charlie Barnet, Duke Ellington, Dizzy Gillespie, and Woody Herman are the stuff of legend.

Percy Hughes's ten-piece group at the Flame on Nicollet Avenue in 1954 featured two of the Twin Cities' finest vocalists of the day. Left to right, Eddie Washington, piano; Dick Mayes and Judy Perkins, vocal; Marv Dahlgren, drums and vibes; Howard (Joe) Williams, bass; Percy Hughes, alto sax; Duffy Goodlow, trumpet; Woodson Bush, alto sax; Stan Haugesag, trombone; Irv Williams, tenor sax.

Later Minnesota musicians also went on the road in traveling bands. Bob Crea, Mickey McClain, Bobby Peterson, Brian Grivna, Bruce Paulson, and Jay Goetting played with Buddy Rich; trumpeter Tom Nygaard, saxman Dick Pendleton, and trombonist George Myers traveled with Herman; saxophonist Jeff Ostlund moved with Herman and Maynard Ferguson; Gordy Johnson also played with Ferguson; Bill Blakkestad, a Rich disciple, played with Stan Kenton; Arnie Ness turned down a trumpet chair with Kenton but did a stint with Ralph Marterie; Wolverines cofounder Dave Sletten traveled with the Artie Shaw group; drummer George Avaloz subbed for Buddy Rich on a date. Steve Wright and drummer Gary Gauger did stints with the Airmen of Note; Gary Berg was with Jimmy Dorsey; high-note specialist Buddy Brisbois from Edina recorded and toured with Kenton (as well as doing a lot of studio work).

Trumpeters Jack Coan and Don Specht and trombonist Stan Haugesag were members of the Bruce Dybvig Orchestra that entered and won *Look* magazine's national competition in 1946. Most of the band's young players came from Minneapolis South, Central, Southwest, and Washburn high schools and were fifteen to seventeen years old. The band started out under Sherman Hector, who had a bunch of Basie charts, but as the band was breaking up, Dybvig and his mentor, Frank Lewis, who was with the navy band, took over and wrote experimental arrangements along with Specht. Lewis played with the Percy Hughes band but left the Twin Cities shortly thereafter for New York with George Hudson. The Dybvig band won the preliminary round in Chicago and went on to New York for the finals. "We started in Carnegie Hall, and it's been downhill ever since," quipped Haugesag. "It was quite an honor. The band was very popular for a few years." Dybvig booked groups into Twin Cities locations and Breezy Point and Bar Harbor resorts in northern Minnesota. Alto sax man Johnny Bothwell fronted the band for a tour, but his failure to pay the musicians led to its demise shortly afterward.

In 1956 *Minneapolis Tribune* columnist Will Jones wrote in a "where are they now" piece that no Dybvig big band members continued to make a living in music, an assertion that was not quite accurate since several members were emerging on the local jazz scene. Jones said that leader Dybvig had probably suffered more than any of his players. "I've just come from my psychiatrist. He says there's nothing wrong with me, and I've given up the idea of committing suicide," said Dybvig. "I want to get

Look magazine's All-America Amateur Swing Band in 1946 was led by Bruce Dybvig (standing at front). Musicians, ages fifteen to eighteen, included drummer Jack Cottrell (not pictured); Paul Sanders, bass; Paul Katruud, piano; Tinkie Ross, vocalist; John Kohler, French horn; trumpets (left to right) Phil Linwick, Jerry Steiner, Dick Zemlin, Don Specht, Jack Coan; trombones: Duane Solem, Stan Haugesag, Darly Barnett, John Roth; saxes: Jack Wellnitz, Lynn Olsen, Bob O'Connell, Don Marveson, Wayne Herhold.

Musicians from *Look* magazine's 1946 award-winning Dybvig band found work, usually in smaller combinations. Northern Minnesota's Bar Harbor was a popular spot for vacationers and music lovers. Pictured in 1950 are, left to right, Jack Cottrell, Stu Anderson, Dirk Fischer, Jack Wellnitz, Bruce Dybvig, Clare Fischer, Dick Zemlin, and Jerry Bergmann.

out of the bandleader business—for good." He bounced around in the music and business worlds but remained frustrated.

Another local big band, the Denny Murphy Band, drew its members from Roosevelt High School's swing band in 1952. Arnie Ness played lead trumpet and helped Edina's Bud Brisbois learn to read music. The band played for school dances, but Murphy decided to get some real gigs. They soon played Saturday nights at the Pillsbury Settlement House, every other Sunday night at St. Matthew's Catholic Church in St. Paul, and Fridays at other high schools. Ness said, "We worked quite a bit and made some good money. Somehow the band kept together after high school, as Denny started importing other good players to fill some spots." Some local notables that played in the Murphy Band include pianists Mickey McClain and Dan Davidson, bassist Jim Hughart, and pianist-arranger-trumpet player John Zdechlik. The band played for the last time in 1957 at a recording session at Kay Bank Studios. Murphy was drafted, and the players went their separate ways.

The Rod Aaberg Band came along a little later, drawing trumpet players Ness, Zdechlik, and Wayne Timmerman from the defunct Murphy Band. It was another award winner, taking sixth place in a national competition for best new college big band of 1960. That same year, Aaberg's band along with Percy Hughes, Harry Blons, Doc Evans, Bob Crea, Willie

Trumpet player–bandleader Rod Aaberg tapped the top talent in the Twin Cities for his big band. Back row: Connie Villers, drums; piano, bass, unknown; trumpets: Jack Coan, Arne Ness, Bob Shannon; trombones: unknown, Stan Haugesag, Pat Rian, Jim tenBensel; saxes: Roy Johnson, Don George, Jack Cooper, Norm Staska.

Glad Olinger's band was noted for its driving beat and fine arrangements. At the Lowry Hotel's Terrace Room, Minneapolis, in 1942 are drummer Ernie Charleston, Jack Nowicki, Don Schirmer, Ray Johnson, Buzzy Goff, Dale Olinger, Bill Vanderlick, Tippy Morgan, Frank Pentranton, Bill Bell, Glad Olinger, and Wes Howard.

Peterson, and the Pettiford-Hector combo played for the "Parade of Jazz" at Minneapolis's parade grounds. Years later, Aaberg left town after allegedly bilking clients in a phony gold investment scheme. (Former members of Aaberg's aggregations formed an alumni band, and in 2004, saxophonist Don George acquired the Aaberg library and began the Bellagala Big Band. The 2010 version of the band featured, among others, trombonists Dave Graf and Jim tenBensel, drummer Joe Pulice, saxman Russ Peterson, pianist Ron Seaman, and Steve Blons on guitar. George died in 2010.)

One big orchestra popular in the Swing Era in the Twin Cities was headed by locals Glad and Dale Olinger. The brothers' star-studded band featured Tom Morgan, on lead alto, who later went with Billy May and ultimately became an A&R (artists and repertoire liaison) man for Capitol Records. "I would say even today, it was very progressive swing music. The arrangements that Jack Nowicki wrote were really quite advanced," said Morgan. "Then Dale Olinger wrote some arrangements that were even closer to jazz than Jack's were . . . There was a musicians' dance at the Coliseum Ballroom. To us, it was a battle of bands. When we went in there with a kid band, we determined that we were going to go in there and knock 'em apart . . . From the first four notes we played of the intro, we knew the band was cookin'. It really swung. Some of the older guys came up and were really nice to us, saying, 'Hey, you guys are playing something.'"

The Olinger band paralleled Benny Goodman's use of mixed racial groups in the thirties by hiring Ernie Charleston, a highly respected black drummer. Drum solos were all the rage then, so Ernie worked up a flashy chart on "Clap Hands! Here Comes Charlie!" It tore up the dance crowds. The band opened the Prom Ballroom in 1941. "Younger musicians started coming around the bandstand to dig us, guys like Bobby Crea and Russ Moore, Tom Talbert, and Bill Blakkestad," recalled Tippy Morgan.

Morgan said he developed his respect for jazz in the Twin Cities belatedly: "I think if I'd have grown up in Minnesota fifteen years later, I would have stayed. Something happened between 1950 and 1960. It got modern. It got contemporary. I never felt that as a kid. I always felt it was a kind of a Spartan existence. A 'Don't go to the movies on Sunday' kind of thing. I always resented it."

Being on the road could be dangerous for big bands that traveled hundreds of miles between engagements. Trumpet player Red Sievers's group was returning from a one-nighter in Marshalltown, Iowa, in October 1941 when their bus was sideswiped by an oncoming cattle truck near Steele Center, Minnesota. Killed instantly were Sievers, age thirty-two, and five others. Among the slightly injured were bassist Cliff Johnson, Don Hallberg, James Leverett, and Joseph Ostberg, all sitting on the right side of the bus. Guitarist Jack Kryzinski said, "Four of us quit the band a few days before. Red had the job in Iowa, but we took another job at a saloon in St. Paul. Those things happened. I'd had enough of this coming home at two or three in the morning." Another time, Sievers "drove into an embankment, hit a telephone pole, and turned over into the yard of a Polish farmer where they'd just finished a wedding reception. There was

Jam sessions and informal concerts were much more the order of the day in the 1950s and '60s. Drummer Russ Moore, an official of the Twin Cities' musicians' union, is shown with bassist Denny Burgess, saxman Gary Berg, and pianist Skip Christman (not visible).

still food out, and he invited the musicians to help themselves. Between accidents and rubber checks from ballroom operators, you had to laugh to keep your sanity," said Kryzinski.

Another young trumpeter, Dick Whitbeck of Bloomington, started with a half dozen of his pre–high school classmates rehearsing Glenn Miller arrangements. He augmented the band, and it became the Blue Diamonds in the 1960s. "We had a lot of really crummy stock [arrangements], but the publishing companies came out with some good stuff," said Whitbeck. "Drummer Terry Waddell was the only writer on the band." Waddell went on to become music director for singer Eddie Arnold. Among the other players were trombonist Tom Keith, the steel-chopped Tom Howard, who had been a member of the famed NORAD band in

Colorado, and guitarist Jim Mansfield. "We rehearsed in laundromats and pizza joints to raise money for charts and put the pay right back," said Whitbeck. The band later became the Dick Whitbeck big band. Whitbeck was staff musician and music director at the Tryone Guthrie Theater for twelve years, and in the 1980s he booked the Carlton Celebrity Room in Bloomington.

One of the hardest-working big bands of the 1970s and '80s was the Wolverines Classic Jazz Orchestra, founded by Ted Unseth in 1973. Consistent personnel made it possible to re-create quality replications of historic jazz-band sounds of the earlier years. The band started playing Sunday nights at Minneapolis's Longhorn Saloon as well as picking up a lot of out-of-town gigs. Since they played for the door, it was commonplace for each player to go home with ten or fifteen dollars a night. They scored a steady engagement at the Commodore Hotel's Speakeasy Room in St. Paul. "Most nights the place was completely packed," said Unseth, "and the dance floor scene was the best—old couples doing authentic steps from the twenties and thirties, young urbanites out there doing it because 'everyone else is doing it,' and free-spirit hippie-types surfing through the thick of it." Twenties trumpet sensation Jabbo Smith joined the Wolverines as a featured player, and Rook Ganz appeared on a 1978 recording. Local jazz greats Eddie Berger and Bob Crea also subbed. Original band member Dave Sletten said the Wolverines was "really a grand experiment. Looking back, one would have to credit Ted Unseth as an idealistic leader and motivator for the project who accomplished the most when he had young, unorthodox players that were willing to listen, learn, and copy the old musical styles without giving thought to financial concerns." Unseth was at the helm until 1980, when he entered into a partnership with drummer Brett Forberg and his parents. As swing and more modern music crept into the repertoire, so did conflict. After a time, with two separate bands, one for the classic sounds that Unseth wanted, the partnership dissolved. Unseth formed De Stijlistics, later called the Americana Classic Jazz Ensemble. The Forbergs retained the Wolverines name on the other, more modern band. Unseth moved to Washington, DC, in 1990 but later returned to the Twin Cities and released a five-disk set of archival material.

Nostalgia was again the centerpiece when Red Wolfe formed Echoes of Ellington in the early seventies. He had played trumpet with the top Dixie

Dave Sletten, a cohost of KBEM's *Twin Cities Jazz Remembered,* was an early driving force in the Wolverines Classic Jazz Orchestra. He toured with the Artie Shaw Orchestra and played with such diverse groups as Manfredo Fest, the Minnesota Orchestra, and touring Broadway shows.

musicians of the thirties and jammed aboard the *Mississippi Queen* riverboat into the forties. Bassist Dick Norling remembered that "Red had a little wind-up phonograph, and whenever we could we'd skip school and go down by Lake Hiawatha and smoke cigarettes and play jazz music, usually Bob Crosby's Bobcats." Wolfe led the band at the Gay '90s in 1952–53 when Glide Snyder first brought in "exotic" dancers to augment the vaudeville-like show. Wolfe, whose favorites were always Louis Armstrong and Harry James, put together an eleven-piece band for some experimental recording. He used Reuben Ristrom, Dick Bortolussi, Dick Norling, Butch Thompson, Jeanne Peterson, and Percy Hughes, among others. The tapes, which featured a lot of overdubbing, never left the studio because Wolfe found it too expensive to pay benefits and licensing fees.

Wolfe and Percy Hughes were honored in 1985 when Governor Rudy Perpich recognized them for keeping jazz alive in Minnesota and when the Twin Cities' mayors proclaimed Red Wolfe and Percy Hughes Day that year. Trombonist Dave Graf, writing for the Twin Cities Jazz Society's newsletter, said, "Red began Ellington Echoes as a lark, transcribing and arranging a few Ellington-associated small-group numbers for an eight-piece band. But the idea had probably been brewing in his mind for quite a while." Some of the tunes were from recordings that Red and Norling had gotten excited about as teenagers. The original band, which made its formal debut in 1986, was made up of Wolfe, trumpet; Percy Hughes and Russ Peterson, reeds; Gene Bird, trombone; Stan Hall on piano; Al Closmore, guitar; Dick Norling, bass; and Dick Bortolussi, drums. Hughes took over Echoes of Ellington after Wolfe died in 1991. Hughes said that "when Red died, it was like losing a blood brother. We had become very close. He'd call me [for engagements] and I would call him whenever we could add another horn."

Bandleader Percy Hughes's career spans many decades. His father and uncles had moved to the Twin Cities at the urging of early Minnesota player Tela Burt, with whom they had served in France during World War I. Percy attended Minneapolis schools, and when he was twelve, Boyd Atkins moved in next door: "I found out he was a famous musician, and he knew I was learning clarinet, so he invited me to come watch him write music and things like that, and then I was allowed to go to eight or ten rehearsals up on Thirty-eighth and Fourth Avenue. We called it the Minnesota Club." Hughes started playing on a C-melody sax that was once Burt's. His first teacher was Jeanette Dorsey at Pillsbury Settlement House: "Oh, she was such a wonderful person. Very laid back, never mean, I never heard her get mad at us. We were fumbling kids you know." At Pillsbury, "Oscar [Pettiford] would come in every so often, probably because Miss Dorsey asked him as a favor. We played Legion ball together for about one week. He hurt his finger and walked off the field and [later] became the world's greatest . . . I should have followed him. He was heads and heels over any of us." Hughes remembered that Margie Pettiford would help the saxophone players and that Rook Ganz and Dave Faison were also seen around Pillsbury.

One of the great local bands of the early 1940s was the U.S. Navy group at Wold-Chamberlin Field, which brought Irv Williams to the Twin Cities and nurtured several other players who would become fixtures around Minneapolis and St. Paul. Saxes (left to right): Granville Mathews, Irv Williams, Woodson Bush, Frank Lewis; piano: Eddie Washington; bass: Howard Williams; drums: Bobby Crittendon; trumpets: Duffy Goodlow, Kenneth Tyler, Hensley Hall; trombones: Oliver Rhodes, Leon Wilson.

During World War II, Hughes heard about the U.S. Navy Band stationed at Wold-Chamberlin Field and made a point to know the players there. Over the years he put together some outstanding bands and had the chance to go on the road backing North Dakota songstress Peggy Lee. He abandoned that opportunity when he learned the group's itinerary called for an extensive tour of the South: "When I came out of the service, I swore no way would I go down south again." In 1954, Hughes found a great "day gig" carrying mail for the U.S. Postal Service. "Carrying mail was the perfect day job for me," he said. "It was good exercise and I enjoyed the people on my route. When I had the opportunity to retire at sixty, I jumped at the chance to devote myself full time to music."

Hughes's band played Bar Harbor near Brainerd, Leigh Kamman's concert series *They Call it Jazz,* and the Treasure Inn on Rice Street on St. Paul's north side. His singers were Hughes's wife, Judy Perkins, and Dick Mayes. The band also played the Flame on Nicollet Avenue until it became a country and western place. "In 1956, I had to reduce the size of my band," said Hughes. "I saw TV start to kill the nightclubs. I went to the Point Supper Club with a quintet and stayed seventeen years, until it burned down." The guitarist on that band was Jack Kryzinski. "I was the first to take the place of a piano," he said. "If you didn't have a piano player, you didn't have a job." He played four years at the Point in Golden Valley and was later replaced by guitarist Welton "Barney" Barnett, and when Hughes switched back to piano players, Tom Slobodzian, Gordy Gladman, and Hubert Eaves each held the keyboard chair.

Hughes received the 1983 Minnesota Black Music Award, the William Griffin Performing Arts Award, and induction into both the Minnesota Jazz Hall of Fame and Music Hall of Fame. Hughes kept playing music and tennis, which he continued to coach well into his eighties.

Tom Talbert, another important big band leader in the Twin Cities, grew up when a thirty-two-story skyscraper, the Foshay Tower, dominated the Minneapolis skyline. Biographer Bruce Talbot found that building an apt metaphor for Talbert's work: "Elegant, confident, original, beautifully constructed, and overshadowed and almost concealed by the grander, the gaudier, and the fashionable, with all that last term implies. A striking piece of Americana, and well worth celebrating."

Veteran saxophonist Percy Hughes found his dream job as a mailman, a position that allowed him to play evenings and weekends and retire early. Here he greets U.S. Senate candidate Clark MacGregor in 1970.

Talbert, born in 1924 at Lake Minnetonka's Crystal Bay, moved to Minneapolis at age nine. Like so many future musicians, his jazz appetite was nurtured by late-night broadcasts from around the country and by buying records. Chester Groth, Hugh Brown, and Del Weibel were early teachers, and young Talbert began to experiment with arranging. At eighteen, he

Many of the Twin Cities' top players and singers graced the stage of the Point Supper Club in Golden Valley, but Percy Hughes reigned supreme. Beginning in 1956, under the ownership of Larry Hort, and later for Herb Klein, he played there for seventeen years. Left to right: Jack Bertelsen, Hughes, Judy Perkins, Howard Williams, Welton Barnett.

formed a band and got a one-nighter at the Marigold Ballroom. When the bass player in the group with four brass, four saxes, and rhythm didn't show, trumpeter Ira Pettiford called his brother Oscar to fill in. Soon, Oscar walked across the dance floor with his bass, no cover, and played the rest of the gig. Later, Oscar would appear on Talbert's recording, *Bix Duke Fats*. Talbot said he regularly used black musicians in 1942, something that attracted little attention at the time.

Talbert continued to write for his eleven-piece group and found work around the Midwest until 1943, when he was drafted. After the service, he ran several big bands before heading west. He and his partner, Margaret Hartigan, moved into the Harvey Hotel on Santa Monica Boulevard, a musicians' hangout. He recruited some excellent players for recording, including his friend from Minneapolis days, Ronnie Rochat on trumpet. Decades later, Minnesota arranger-bandleader Maria Schneider said Talbert's

Tommy McGovern, his sister Patty, and many others played the Nicollet Hotel in Minneapolis in the early forties. Its first incarnation in the late nineteenth century gave way to the wrecking ball and a new, modern hotel in 1924. Today, it's a parking lot.

late-1940s chart of "I've Got You Under My Skin" was "genius writing—the figure that's behind the melody at the beginning and the way he brings it back again at the end, and also the contrast of the piece—it's just so daring." She compared Talbert's writing to Ellington, Billy Strayhorn, and her own mentor, Gil Evans.

Talbert tried New York City in the fifties and recorded two of his most successful albums, *Wednesday's Child,* with vocalist Patty McGovern, and *Bix Duke Fats.* Frustrated with the scene, he reluctantly returned to Minneapolis, later noting that he had "always hated Minneapolis" and "went back with a bit of a chip on my shoulder." He fronted a big band that featured, among others, Russ Moore, George Myers, Arnie Ness, and Irv Williams. They worked around Minneapolis until Talbert escaped to a dairy farm in Wisconsin. Musical wanderlust caught up with him again, and in 1975 he returned to California where, always the optimist, he worked until he had a stroke. He established a music scholarship, of which an early recipient was Maria Schneider, and died at age eighty in 2005.

Schneider, born in 1960, got her early musical training in Windom, Minnesota, before studying at the University of Minnesota. She has become an award-winning and highly respected composer and orchestra leader. Her first piano teacher, Evelyn Butler, taught her "stride style"—a jazz piano style evolved partially from ragtime. A friend in the university dorm turned her on to the more contemporary sounds of McCoy Tyner and Herbie Hancock. "I couldn't believe how the left hand had changed," she said. "You were no longer playing bass notes in the left hand, but there were all these quartile modern voicings, and it freed up the bass to move on its own . . . That was such a revelation."

Trombonist Bob Brookmeyer, a clinician at the university, became one of Schneider's mentors. So did Gil Evans. She studied piano with Manfredo Fest while still in the Twin Cities, although she has never considered herself an instrumental soloist. She left the Twin Cities for New York in 1985 to study before she formed her own orchestra in 1992. Schneider has written several commissioned works, including *Scenes from Childhood, Willow Lake,* based on her childhood in rural Minnesota, which debuted at the Monterey Jazz Festival. In 2005 Schneider's orchestra won a Grammy in the Best Large Jazz Ensemble Album category for *Concert in the Garden.* The album was pressed in a limited run of ten thousand copies and sold solely online, without conventional retail distribution.

Schneider's orchestra played regularly at Visiones in New York. (Another midwesterner, sax player Dick Oatts, who called the Twin Cities home from 1972 to 1977, was a section leader nearby at the Village Vanguard with the Thad Jones–Mel Lewis band.) Schneider says she doesn't feel pressure being a role model for far-too-rare young female composers, but she realizes that her presence has an effect on people when she goes to schools: "You just get a sense how young girls are looking at you. For me, when I was at Minnesota, I think my junior or senior year at the U, the band of Toshiko [Akiyoshi] came through and played at Orchestra Hall. And [seeing] her in front . . . the power she had with that band and the command really had an effect on me."

Traveling big bands and dance orchestras frequently played at dance halls outside Minneapolis. A popular spot on Lake Minnetonka from the forties into the sixties was the notable Down Beat at Spring Park, a destination reached by boat or car. Dick Bruzik, a drummer who ran the Down Beat,

As new hotels and commercial development went up at the curve on Nicollet Avenue in Minneapolis, the old Marigold Ballroom came down on May 24, 1975.

backed trombonist George Myers and a trombone ensemble that grew into a big band featuring some of the Twin Cities' top players. It included Bob Crea on bari sax, trumpeter Arnie Ness, Percy Hughes, and a young Bobby Lyle. Leigh Kamman, Dick Driscoll, and Herb Schoenbohm did remote radio broadcasts from the club, part of a programming package they tried unsuccessfully to promote on KQRS, then KUXL. "Boy, that band sounded good," Irv Williams said. "George wrote some nice stuff for that band."

Lake Minnetonka's Excelsior Amusement Park also boasted a ballroom, known in some circles as Big Reggie's for its proprietor. Jeanne Arland (Peterson) sang there in 1939, and touring bands such as Glen Gray and the Casa Loma Orchestra played one-nighters. Years later, the young Edina group known as the Dixieland Ramblers also graced its stage.

Finally, although it would be a stretch to call Jules Herman's orchestra a "jazz band," many jazz players cycled through Herman's group over the thirty-five years he led it. It was one of the area's last regionally traveling dance bands, or "territory bands." Herman, who played trumpet with Lawrence Welk's band in the 1930s, made his home base at the Prom Ballroom on University Avenue in St. Paul. On the Prom's huge stage, it was not uncommon to see farmers in overalls dancing with their wives on Sunday nights as announcer Charlie Boone took the cue precisely at eight in the evening and WCCO listeners across the Midwest heard the words, "Let's go dancing at the Prom." Herman's wife, Lois Best, who was Lawrence Welk's first "Champagne Lady," played the Hammond B-3. Dave Sletten once remarked that "every musician in town has helped haul that organ in for the job."

12

The Singers

"All the intelligence and talent in the world can't make a singer. The voice is a wild thing. It can't be bred in captivity. It is a sport, like the silver fox. It happens."
—Willa Cather, *novelist*

From the earliest days of jazz in the Twin Cities, vocalists have sung melodies in front of bands and provided the focal point for the musicians who accompany them. Singers can define the band sound or get lost in the musical shuffle. From Joe Roberts's vocal stylings with the Slatz Randall band of the twenties to Debbie Duncan with the Adi Yeshaya band of the nineties to Charmin Michelle with the Jerry O'Hagan Orchestra in the new century, singers have commanded the spotlight.

While the distaff side dominates the field, visiting singer and bandleader Billy Eckstine played Washington Avenue's Key Club in the 1950s. He encouraged drummer George Avaloz to expand his horizons by checking out the Chicago music scene. After a long stint with Eckstine, Avaloz came home to accompany some of the Twin Cities' finest singers, including Debbie Duncan and Shirley Witherspoon. Witherspoon sang a year with the Ellington band and would return to pay tribute to Billie Holiday and Bessie Smith. Avaloz, who worked with Witherspoon on and off for more than four decades, said she was "definitely one of the better singers to come out of here . . . She sang with a lot of feeling, and she was a very soulful person."

North Dakota's Miss Peggy Lee, born Norma Egstrom in 1920, traveled to the Twin Cities around 1940 hoping to find work after an unsuccessful

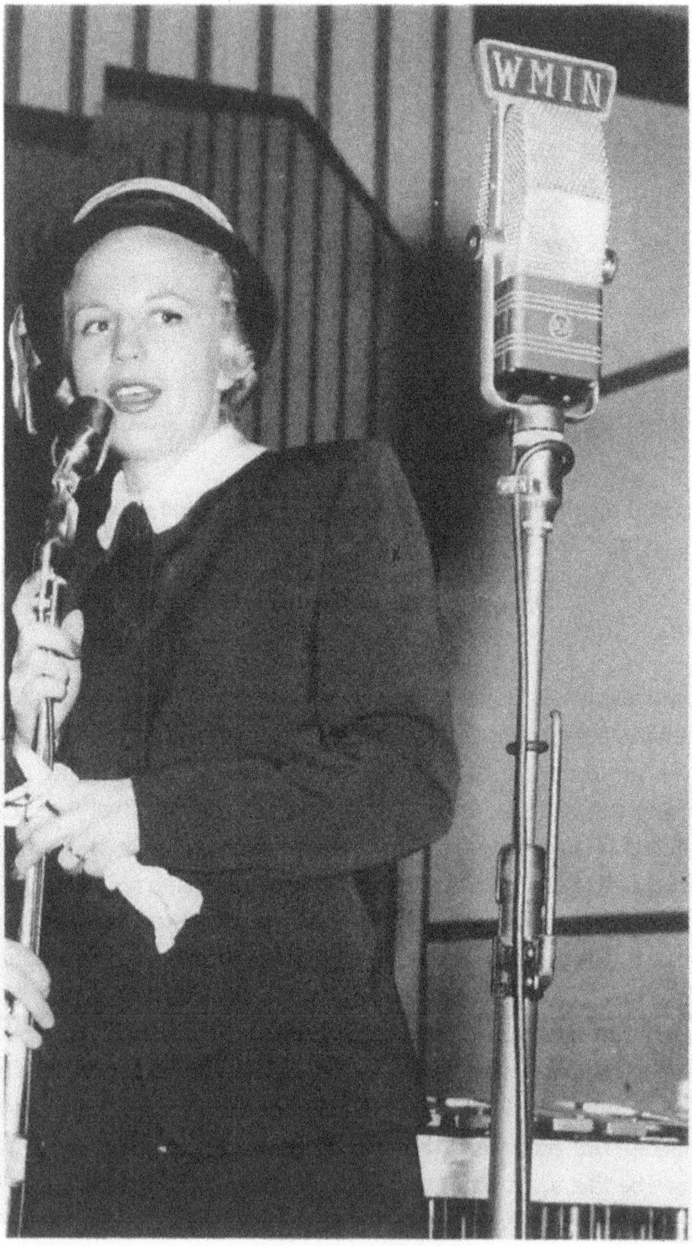

Songstress Peggy Lee—long after shedding her North Dakota moniker, Norma Egstrom—sings at Mitch's. The Mendota nightspot was a must-stop for visiting celebrities.

venture to California. Jeanne Arland (Peterson), who was dating her future husband, pianist Willie Peterson, and singing at the Athletic Club, would sometimes "go over to listen. When Willie saw me, he'd ask Peggy to sing, 'I Dream of Jeannie.' She was with Sev Olson, who had the orchestra at the old Radisson Hotel. She sang so well!" said Peterson. "I was jealous of her. She was quiet, reserved, didn't blow her own horn at all, but so able to do her craft. She was a good-looking lady, too." Peterson recalled that Lee lived on a shoestring: "She had a show on KSTP just before she was going to leave town, and they asked me to replace her. I went over to watch her. She told me she needed earrings. I went to downtown St. Paul and bought her a ten-cent pair of earrings." Jeanne's husband loaned Lee money to leave town for a successful audition in Chicago with Benny Goodman. Today, Jeanne Arland Peterson—and her daughter Patty Peterson—are counted among the top Twin Cities vocalists.

Also singing in the Swing Era were the locally born and nationally famous Andrews Sisters. They began their close-harmony swing and boogie-woogie vocalizing careers in radio and talent contests in the Twin Cities. The Andrews Sisters made an unsuccessful 1937 recording before hitting the big time, thanks to manager Lou Levy (not the jazz pianist who would later call the Twin Cities home). Sometimes called "the new Peggy Lee," St. Louis Park native Maud Hixson has attracted the attention of singers and critics. In 2005, she recorded with one of the few male vocalists in the Twin Cities, Arne Fogel. Fogel is also a producer and entertainment historian.

Singer Debbie Duncan, called a "Perpetual Outstanding Performer" at the Minnesota Music Awards, is one of the most visible performers on the current scene. She landed in the Twin Cities by way of Memphis, Detroit, and Los Angeles. Duncan has sung with many of the top names in the business and appeared in the 2008 production of *Blues in the Night* at the Ordway Theater.

Lineups from years long gone included vocalist Barbara Hughes, singing in 1940 with Vinnie's Dixieland Band. The group featured Vince Bastien, Don Thompson, Larry Brakke, and Lloyd Horton. Performing still earlier—in 1925—at the Orpheum with Isham Jones was "top jazz vocalist" Jane Green. Kelly Stoneman sang on WDGY in the 1930s with Lester Young, Rook Ganz, Walter Lear, and Popeye Booker.

Patty McGovern started out accompanied by brother Tommy; she joined the Honey Dreamers in 1950 and headed for New York. Her finest recording was "Wednesday's Child" with Tom Talbert's band. She was married for fifteen years to broadcaster Leigh Kamman.

Some Twin Cities vocalists left for greener pastures. Patty McGovern, sister of pianist-bandleader Tommy McGovern, sang with his band at the Nicollet Hotel before World War II and later was a student with Leigh Kamman at the U of M. They married and spent time in Duluth. In 1950 she was the lucky one of more than fifty to audition for a spot in the Honey Dreamers, a vocal group beginning at St. Olaf College and loosely patterned after the Hi-Lo's. Kamman's friend Arthur Ward told Stan Kenton, who was playing at Coffman Union, "You've got to hear this group." Kenton offered to take the Honey Dreamers on the road with his band but they turned him down and went instead to New York. Making the trek with Patty in 1950 was husband Leigh Kamman. Shortly after arriving there, Kamman copped a position with Harlem's WOV radio. *Billboard* magazine proclaimed Patty McGovern's 1956 recording of "Wednesday's Child" with Tom Talbert "a sleeper... one of the day's better vocalists with appeal to both 'cool' and pop cults."

Bandleader Jules Herman's daughter Bonnie would often sit in with her dad's band at the Prom Ballroom and other halls around the Midwest. Jules said, "Bonnie made a name for herself with the former Hi-Lo's. She became the lead singer for them when they changed the name and became the famous Singers Unlimited." Bonnie also did commercial and jingle recording.

In the late eighties jazz Grammy nominee Karrin Allyson spent several years in the Twin Cities. She honed her skills before going on to larger and greener pastures.

Lila Ammons, a member of the famous Ammons family that included boogie-woogie pianist Albert and tenor-sax great Gene, arrived in the Twin Cities from New York in 1997 with a dozen years of classical training and experience on her résumé. She began transitioning into the jazz scene and has appeared at many of the top night spots.

The male vocalist category in the Twin Cities over the years has been populated by just a handful of regulars. Many of them are instrumentalists who also sing. One of the most talented local male vocalists was Dick Mayes. Dickie shared the vocal spotlight in the forties with Percy Hughes's wife, Judy Perkins, at the Flame on Nicollet Avenue. Later, Mayes was featured with George Myers's band at the Down Beat Club near Lake

One-time Twin Citian Dave Frishberg came to town to collaborate with vocalist Connie Evingson on her recording *Little Did I Dream*, featuring songs by lyricist-pianist Frishberg and also involving reed man Dave Karr.

Minnetonka. He did several extended engagements at the Sheraton-Ritz's Golliwog Lounge.

Bruce Henry has what Andrea Canter, on the website Jazz Police, has called "perhaps the most easily identified male voice in Twin Cities jazz." Drummer George Avaloz is an accomplished singer, influenced by his former boss Billy Eckstine. Dennis Spears has been showcased as a soloist but perhaps is best known for ensemble work with Moore by Four, which also features Connie Evingson. Rio Nido was a vocal trio born in the seventies and fronted by singer Prudence Johnson. It took on the jazz flavor of Lambert, Hendricks, and Ross and added a pop element. Big bands such as Bellagala regularly feature Sinatra-influenced crooners like Bob Glenn and Vic Volare.

In its more than six decades of existence, the Four Freshmen have had just three lead singers, including suburban Apple Valley–raised Brian Eichenberger. He began singing with the Frosh in 1996 at age twenty. The Harley-driving Eichenberger also plays guitar and piano and is a musical arranger for the group. He studied at Phil Mattson's School for Music Vocations in Creston, Iowa.

Pianist Jim Trost joined a trio backing Toni Lee Scott at Herb's in downtown Minneapolis in the 1960s. "Toni was a very good jazz vocalist, but her real appeal was as a torch singer," noted Trost. "She sang sad ballads about broken dreams and unrequited love in a spell-binding style that thrilled audiences, particularly women . . . Toni had lost a leg in a motorcycle accident . . . This fact, coupled with her choice of music and her unquestioned dramatic ability, allowed her to personalize the pathos of the song lyrics, making them her and every woman's story. I have never known another singer to do this so well and so convincingly."

Carole Martin was a mainstay at clubs around the twin towns in the sixties and beyond. She now performs only rare evenings at son-in-law Kenny Horst's Artists' Quarter. Carole recorded *Pieces of Dreams* in 2005, which the *Star Tribune*'s Jon Bream called "the finest jazz-vocal CD from the Twin Cities in many a moon." Judi Donaghy is a musical jill-of-all-trades. She worked seven years with Bobby McFerrin's Voicestra and is a regular in Twin Cities clubs.

Two vocalists, Roberta Davis and Doris Hines, together were subjects of a Dave Sletten–Kent Hazen interview on KBEM. Davis, whose roots are in gospel music, found jazz relatively late in life. After time at the Berklee school in Boston and tours of Europe, Hines recently celebrated her eighty-fifth birthday at the Dakota with a guest appearance by her son, Gary, of Sounds of Blackness fame, and by members of the Peterson family.

Guitarist Reuben Ristrom relates that his favorite once-local singer is Shirley Forwood, who moved to Florida and then to Colorado Springs with husband Dan Matsche. Forwood sang in the Twin Cities in the 1960s backed by Ristrom, pianist Hal Lichterman, and others. In the same decade, Geri Mitchum sang at Herb's Bar with the Floyd Morris Trio and drummer-husband Bill Hobbs. *Minneapolis Tribune* scribe Will Jones described her as "an ominous satire of most of the mannered girl coolsters you've ever seen (and a few hotsters thrown in), with occasional fleeting glimpses of her own unique swinging self."

Vocalist Carole Martin's 2005 album *Pieces of Dreams* was described by *Star Tribune* writer Jon Bream as "the finest jazz-vocal CD from the Twin Cities in many a moon."

The plethora of practicing talented vocalists in the Twin Cities in the past and today may be a mixed blessing. In the estimation of drummer Phil Hey, it contributes to the slow pace of jazz bookings. On the club scene, singers always get more stage time than instrumentalists, he says, because vocal music is easier for audiences to grasp than complex instrumental playing. "I know saying this is going to get me in trouble," he muses, "but singers are running the show... How can I put this? I don't want to lose work."

13

Jazz on the Air

"I don't stay out late, don't care to go, I'm home about eight,
just me and my radio."
—Andy Razaf, "Ain't Misbehavin'"

Since the 1920s, music has been integral to radio programming. The University of Minnesota received the state's first broadcasting license in 1922 as WLB (now the country's oldest noncommercial station still on the air as KUOM, "Where Music Matters Most"). WAMD (now KSTP)—"Where All Minneapolis Dances"—made its inaugural broadcast in 1925 from the Marigold Ballroom on Nicollet Avenue and Grant Street and soon presented dance band music programs five nights a week. By 1928 it boasted the largest live-radio staff orchestra in the nation.

Throughout the Roaring Twenties, radio stations featured live broadcasts of music from the Radisson, St. Paul, and Nicollet hotels as well as from ballrooms. Some programs were fed to stations well beyond the flagship, which gave the bands increased audiences and name recognition. Airplay also forced groups to expand their repertoires since a more discerning public quickly learned the new tunes of the day.

Trombonist Hal Runyon recalled playing with the well-known big band led by George Osborn, known (mostly behind his back) as "Old Stone Face." Runyon said the job, dating to about 1930, "was a commercial radio job for Phillips 66 . . . emanating from KSTP, which at that time was in the St. Paul Hotel . . . We'd broadcast from there five nights a week. It was the first big radio program that ever came out of the Twin Cities."

According to Frankie Roberts, the musicians' union required that all the Twin Cities radio stations have staff orchestras—no records were played. He and Norvy Mulligan found a lot of work on WCCO. *Noon Highlights,* sponsored by the Hormel meat company, had six half-hour shows a week: "We'd play Lindy's off Fifth and Hennepin 'til 4 AM, then we'd be at WCCO at 8:30 AM, and, later in the day, the Palace Theater. All the bands came into Lindy's. It was 1937. There was a gambling place on the second floor; the Camel's Club was a basement place, where the dance floor had a sewer plate in the middle."

Roberts recalled playing in the forties for WCCO's *Ad Lib Club,* which he said was a misnomer: "It wasn't true. We used arrangements, but some announcers thought it sounded good. We'd do kind of a skit with Bob DeHaven. Sometimes we had to be there at five in the morning; rehearsal was at six." Vince Bastien wrote "skeletal arrangements" of the Dixie tunes, but he credited Roberts's steel-trap memory for the introductions and choruses to all the standards for getting them going. "There's a characteristic movement for the clarinet, the trumpet, and the trombone," said Bastien. "I'd set up what the melody was doing and then have the chord symbol so that each guy could move around in his characteristic fashion." Some musicians were paid by the broadcast and not hired on staff right away. Roberts, Mulligan, and others played on staff from 1937 to 1955. Roberts said in 1959 he was playing rock-and-roll tenor: "Then a couple of New York promoters got the idea of a competition between two radio stations. With Jimmy Robb's band, we'd play a little jazz, but not too much. The buck came first, you know? If you wanted to work."

Jazz radioman Leigh Kamman's interest in radio was piqued as a young teen in the early 1930s when he did odd jobs at the Silver Beach Resort near Glenwood, Minnesota. Late at night and on rainy days he heard the likes of Bessie Smith, Andy Kirk, and Mary Lou Williams on the proprietors' radio. "We'd be all knocked out from the work and went to sleep to that music," he said. Jazz entrepreneur and recording engineer Jerry Newhouse would hold listening sessions for young enthusiasts and led the *Saturday Night Swing Club* on WMIN in the late thirties. Kamman said that Newhouse, a sophisticated record collector, would "expose us to the truth of jazz and its historic accuracy."

In his teens, Kamman got the first of what would be treasured interviews with Duke Ellington at the Coliseum Ballroom at University and

Dean of jazz broadcasters, Leigh Kamman

Lexington in St. Paul. A later rendezvous with the Duke was less positive. Kamman offered Ellington a ride to the St. Paul Hotel, where an interview had been scheduled with KSTP's Don Hawkins. As they approached the hotel elevators, a bellman directed them to the freight elevator. "That was a signal, so we never delivered the interview with Ellington," said Kamman. "We turned and drove Ellington to the Hotel Nicollet, where he was registered and got in without a problem."

Kamman attended the University of Minnesota, where he appeared on KUOM (then WLB). The station was committed to news, agriculture, classical music, and radio drama. Jazz was forbidden. But soon he and Sev Widman started emptying wastebaskets at WMIN, where Kamman was able to do his first jazz broadcast around 1938, titled *Studio Party Wham.* Kamman insisted he and his friends remained "green, unsophisticated, naïve young broadcasters."

World War II brought the possibility of a career jump for Kamman when male broadcast staff members were being drafted. Leigh and friend Ted Lee hitchhiked to Duluth to audition at NBC-affiliate WEBC, the key station of the Arrowhead Network. Kamman learned a lot about radio during his short time there. He did a Saturday night show at 11 PM called *Symphony in Riffs,* after the Benny Carter composition. The live broadcast originated from the upscale Flame Supper Club on London Road and featured such artists as the Anson Weeks Band, Snub Moseley, and Coleman Hawkins. Kamman later found himself nearby in the port city at KDAL, where he worked as promotions manager. With just a half hour a week of programming devoted to jazz, he stayed only a year before returning to the Twin Cities.

Then Kamman put in a five-year stint in the army. "I'm really very lucky," said Kamman. "I became an information specialist and had privileges when a lot of people were sweating it out." Kamman was initially assigned at Fitzsimons General Hospital in Denver, where he later hosted *Clambake in Khaki,* which featured an eighteen-piece jazz band made up of gifted musicians under direction of Hal Hastings (who later conducted *Fiorello* on Broadway). The musicians were from several of the bands of the day, including Jack Teagarden's. The program featured amateur talent and produced some gifted performer-servicemen, including actor Karl Malden.

On discharge in 1946, Kamman went back to the University of Minnesota. He hosted *The Swing Club* on WLOL, as well as a series of fourteen concerts for *We Call It Jazz.* The first program in the series featured Percy Hughes's eight-piece band and singer Judy Perkins. Originating at the Radisson Hotel, it spotlighted such works as "Knocked-out Nocturne," "Fantasy in Moonbeams," and "Ode to a Commode." Hughes remembered, "The schools fell in love with the band thanks to radio . . . Carleton, Hamline, Macalester, the U of M—Leigh opened all the doors for me."

Kamman's smooth voice was becoming more familiar in the Twin Cities as the popular *Dixieland Caravan* was broadcast live from Mitch's in Mendota on WMIN. Eddie Tolck, the drummer and vibraphonist in Harry Blons's Mendota Buzzards, said, "Those were fun days. Anybody

Percy Hughes with singer Judy Perkins, later his wife, played the Depot on North Lexington, St. Paul, in 1947. The club was made up of two refurbished rail coaches.

that meant anything who was in town would be there." Guests included Mel Tormé and Peggy Lee.

By 1948, Kamman was becoming firmly entrenched in Twin Cities radio. He was also feeding local happenings as a stringer for *DownBeat* and *Variety* magazines, even managing to get saxophonist Percy Hughes's band on the cover of a 1950 issue. Jack Tracy, who served as jazz columnist for the *Minnesota Daily* on the university campus, later became editor at *DownBeat*.

Kamman says that a major influence on him as a broadcaster was George Carson Putnam, also from St. Paul Central High School. Putnam began as a twenty-year-old announcer in Minneapolis in 1934 and went on to a highly successful career on both coasts. Columnist Walter Winchell once dubbed Putnam's voice "the best in radio." On the topic of mellifluous tones, Percy Hughes told Chuck Haga of the *Star Tribune,* "Leigh Kamman's instrument is a microphone. There's only one voice like that in this world."

Kamman quickly became a local legend in jazz broadcasting, and as former colleague John Kalbrener said, "Everybody has Leigh Kamman stories. Me, too." Kalbrener recalled sitting in a corner booth with Kamman at the old Market BBQ on the southern edge of downtown Minneapolis when Duke Ellington and some of his players came in after a gig.

The Duke and Kamman would hook up again in New York City, and the broadcaster remembers an unusual meeting with Ellington collaborator Billy Strayhorn there. In their apartment at 106th Street and Central Park West, Leigh and singer Patty McGovern were rehearsing, and their voices could be heard through a painted window that led to an airshaft in their Harlem apartment. Strayhorn heard them and commented positively, introducing himself in an eerie echo emanating from the opening. "Who are you?" asked Kamman. "Billy Strayhorn," came the reply. In New York Leigh would make the club rounds with Horace William Greeley III, an old friend from Duluth who covered the three television networks for *Variety.* "Leigh was the first white guy to dare to broadcast music and interviews on a regular basis from Harlem," said Kalbrener.

Interviewing Ellington was a lifelong endeavor for Kamman: "I decided I would interview him whenever I could, somehow, some place, and I really did that up to the year before he died [in 1974]." Kamman was barely out of high school when he first encountered the Duke. His first jazz interview was with the manager of Chick Webb's swing band at the St. Paul Auditorium. Kamman recalled, "Duke was very cordial to a young, green reporter." Kamman put a microphone in front of Ellington several more times, including once at the Monterey Jazz Festival and again at the Guthrie Theater with Duke's son, Mercer.

In 1956 Kamman returned to the Twin Cities from New York. He worked at WLOL, then at KSTP, where he did *Image, the '60s,* and other programs for NBC's *Monitor.* He hosted live broadcasts from Freddy's with Teddy Wilson, Count Basie, and others. Freddy's opened in 1934 at 605 Second Avenue South as a restaurant only, and in 1959 it moved around the corner to 211 South Sixth Street when Pete Karalis purchased it.

One of Kamman's outstanding broadcasts from Freddy's was during an appearance by Ella Fitzgerald, backed by the Oscar Peterson Trio. Engineer Howard Hefley and Kamman were doing level checks for their broadcast. Kamman had "mentioned to Patty McGovern that Ella was appearing and asked what would she think about doing a lead sheet for 'Mack the Knife,' a popular tune of the day by Kurt Weill and recorded by Louis Armstrong and Bobby Darrin." Ella looked at Patty's sheet and shook her head and handed it to bassist Ray Brown. Kamman thought his idea had been rejected, but when he received the advance song sheet for clearing royalties, there "Mack the Knife" was on the list. That night, Ella performed it on the air. Six weeks later she performed it in Berlin, and it was a smash.

One of Kamman's colleagues in the 1960s was pianist-broadcaster Herb Schoenbohm. Kamman recalls their "adventure at KQRS," when the pair attempted to convince management of the value of a jazz-and-classical-music format. Their effort failed, although the station did a series of live broadcasts produced by Dick Driscoll from Culbertson's in St. Louis Park (formerly the Cotton Club and El Patio). "He's creative as can be," Kamman said of Schoenbohm. Kamman credited him with bringing Brazilian music to the Twin Cities. Schoenbohm's father, who founded Camp Courage, helped fund a visit to the Mayo Clinic by Brazilian pianist Manfredo Fest. Legally blind since birth, Fest hoped to regain his sight. While that was not to be, Fest did find a musical home in the Twin Cities. He went on to play extended gigs at Davey Jones' Locker in the Downtowner Motel and at Irv Schechtman's White House restaurant in Golden Valley.

Schechtman, KQRS, Kamman, and Schoenbohm were prime movers in establishing the short-lived Festival of the Elegant Arts, held at several locations including Dayton's department store's Fifth Floor Gallery. It featured such jazz luminaries as Gerry Mulligan and Stan Getz and was given a financial boost by Hathaway shirts.

Kamman is best known today for his long tenure as host of Minnesota Public Radio's *THE JAZZ IMAGE™*, which had a remarkable run from 1973 to 2007. When he retired, Maryann Sullivan took over the show, but MPR soon cancelled it. This move left a huge gap in local jazz programming. Sullivan moved over to KBEM 88.5, a station affiliated with Minneapolis public schools and devoted to jazz and traffic information. Also on KBEM today, guitarist Steve Blons teams with Michele Jansen for *Jazz and the Spirit*. The program explores both ends of that title, which offers a broad spectrum. It has featured such luminaries as McCoy Tyner, Sonny Rollins, and Al Jarreau talking about the metaphysical aspects of their art.

Outside the immediate Twin Cities, jazz has been an even more difficult commodity to sell on radio or television. In 1958 Eddie Berger had limited success in a very small market, KDUZ in Hutchinson, with a noontime daily show. Short lived though it may have been, it caught the ears of a few fans. Eddie's friends wondered how he dared put such progressive sounds out for listeners more likely to be interested in grain prices and pork belly futures. "Wally Walstad used to listen to it because he said it was incredible for this little town," said Berger. "He said he listened all the time because it was so weird and so outside for that neck of the woods." Aware of his dim prospects at KDUZ—the audience was a fraction of what Leigh Kamman had had in New York City or even after his return to the Twin Cities in '58—Berger moved to Minneapolis for a Hennepin Avenue club stint. He later returned to radio and hosted a jazz show for nearly twenty-five years on KFAI community radio in Minneapolis. Berger, like many aspiring young broadcasters of the day, had attended Minneapolis's Brown Institute (then on East Lake Street) to learn the trade and acquire the requisite FCC broadcaster licenses.

Another player who entered broadcasting after playing music himself was Norvy Mulligan. Following a long hiatus from performing, Mulligan played jazz on KTWN in Anoka for seventeen years before his death in 1985.

Some of Minnesota's jazz radio programming has reached wider audiences. Beginning in 1959, well-known radio personality Franklin Hobbs could be heard nationwide on the late-night post from 10:30 PM until 5 AM at WCCO. While not strictly a jazzer, he picked his own music from the catalogs of artists such as Sinatra, Fitzgerald, and the big bands. *Hobbs House* could be heard around the country on the 50,000-watt station at 830 on the AM dial for two decades. Joe McFarland also did a traditional jazz show on WCCO about the same time.

Garrison Keillor's *Prairie Home Companion* on National Public Radio is known around the United States for its eclectic humor and music. Keillor often features jazz, especially the homegrown variety. Remembering St. Paul

Red Maddock had a well-known sense of humor, but as *DownBeat* reported in the 1940s, "Maddock's band, with the exception of Red himself, was recently canned from the Magic Bar [Minneapolis] because the sidemen were 'not funny enough.'"

musicians that had appeared on his show originating at the Fitzgerald Theater, Keillor tipped his hat to "the late George 'Red' Maddock, an old St. Paul nightclub drummer of whom Chet Atkins said he had the steadiest beat and could propel a band better than anyone he ever heard. God bless you, Red."

Big band and traditional jazz also get airplay on KBEM, a community public radio station linked to the Minneapolis public schools. Pianist Butch Thompson's *Jazz Originals* runs weekly, and Jerry Swanberg's *Big Band Scene* airs for an hour twice a week.

Jazz has more rarely appeared on television. In the 1960s and 1970s pioneers such as WCCO-TV's Bill Carlson, best known as an interviewer, would feature local musicians on the program titled *Something Special.* It gave way to a late Saturday-night variety and talk show, *This Must Be the Place,* that included players who would show up after gigs for a live shot, intermingled with old movies. Carlson frequently featured Dave Rooney's trio on his show at a time when Rooney was moving from Big Al's to Diamond Lil's.

Dating to Eddie Berger's brief jazz sojourn in Hutchinson, a few jazz broadcasts still originate in the Minnesota hinterlands. KMSU at Mankato State University devotes time each week to jazz, some of it syndicated. Henry Busse, Jr., son of 1930s sweet-sounding trumpeter and bandleader Henry Busse, is an emeritus staff member there after bouncing around several small radio markets. Busse mixes other genres with jazz in a nostalgia format. Lona Falenczykowski has been doing her *Ms. Lona Tonight* jazz show as a volunteer since 1985. WTIP, a community radio station on the North Shore, also plays some jazz.

While jazz holds a small niche in broadcast media, jazz enthusiasts have had even fewer places to get in-depth written coverage. The one notable local exception has been the *Mississippi Rag*™. Founded in 1973 by Leslie Johnson, who functioned as editor for thirty-five years before her death in 2009, the *Rag* gained a wide reputation for substantial coverage of traditional jazz. It is an important archive of jazz knowledge. Its tabloid format made it possible to include rare and sometimes unique photos. The magazine has boasted such writers and editors as Butch Thompson (who wrote its first feature article on Max Morath), William Schafer, and Paige Van Vorst. Schafer commented, "*The Mississippi Rag* has contributed . . . by maintaining its fidelity to quality of music, its accuracy, its material; its

Traditional jazz specialist Butch Thompson

historical research has given this entire industry... the journal that has made it grow." It became an online-only entity in 2007 under the leadership of Johnson's husband, retired media man Will Shapira. In 2009, it ceased publication.

Shows featuring jazz and swing music, once staples of radio, are harder to find on the AM and FM dials. Minnesota Public Radio abandoned the genre shortly after Leigh Kamman's departure; San Francisco's KJAZ has passed on; this story repeats in other markets. The current trend toward digital technology and satellite radio is encouraging, but jazz appears lost in the quagmire. Pandora offers a good "customized" music selection on the Internet, and services such as Dish put forth nearly a dozen jazz alternatives, albeit on a menu of hundreds. For the patient listener, jazz is there to be found.

14

Jazz in the New Millennium

"I could spend fifty hours on the last twenty-five years of jazz and still not do it justice."
—KEN BURNS, *documentary filmmaker*

Anyone taking time to skim the formidable list of young musicians now playing in the Twin Cities will see that the future of jazz is in good hands. It is full of up-and-comers with impressive bona fides in training, collaboration, and playing experience.

The Artists' Quarter weekly e-mail newsletter is not the Who's Who of Twin Cities jazz, but perhaps it is a Who Will Be of Twin Cities jazz—if social and economic conditions allow it. Jazz has recently seen the hardest of times since the Great Depression cut down playing opportunities for musicians young and old. Those who have found work play for less remuneration. Some young musicians are even willing to pay clubs for the opportunity to play and, with luck, gain some exposure.

Conditions have definitely changed for aspiring musicians. Even before the new millennium, trombonist Stan Haugesag observed, "Unionism has declined so there are fewer places to find jazz; disc jockeys have replaced live music, and competition is keen for the jobs that are available. Promotion has become the key ingredient for working as any kind of musician." Haugesag noted that one bright spot has been the introduction of jazz programs in high schools and colleges that "provide the means for aspiring players to study and learn all about jazz." The danger is that jazz education becomes an end in itself, and playing and improvising take a back seat to teaching and research.

Some jazz players today remain firmly into their art for the sake of exploration and creation. Avant-garde or free jazz—the new music that developed among players like Ornette Coleman, Charles Mingus, Sun Ra, and a host of others—broke down time and harmony conventions, creating a music less accessible to the mainstream listener yet unleashing a creative energy among its practitioners. Twin Cities free jazz proponent Milo Fine, along with Davu Seru, Steve Gnitka, Scott Newell, John O'Brien, Joe Smith, Anthony Cox, Viv Corringham, Paul Metzger, and others, cares not so much about the audience acceptance as about taking the audience along on a musical and spiritual journey.

Fine, a Twin Cities native who studied percussion informally with his father, Elliot Fine of the Minnesota Symphony Orchestra, teaches at the West Bank School of Music and covers classical, rock, and jazz percussion with a focus on free and improvised music. Fine says that there used to be a "palpable sense that anything was possible" and that people could change the world, a feeling necessary for evolutionary development in every creative endeavor. Considering himself fortunate to have been at the epicenter of free jazz development, Fine says, "Creative necessity rather than careerism was the guiding principle." Fine believes schools are now fueled by the media and an arts bureaucracy that are "gatekeepers, tastemakers, and puppet-masters." When he started his career in 1969, "academia was decades away from even starting to acknowledge the existence" of free jazz. Now, like Dixieland, swing, and bebop, Fine says, "Free jazz has fallen prey to aesthetic codification, opportunism, and the unhealthy business mind-set." He refuses to compromise in order to fill a room: "I don't want to stroke people by playing 'Satin Doll' and a million other standards . . . Listeners have to make an effort."

As the six-night-a-week musicians' gig common in the fifties and sixties has disappeared, "playing for the door"—which many musicians did at Prohibition-era clubs—has returned. Making a living in music, especially in jazz, is difficult, and the proverbial "day gig" has become a standard part of the musician's life.

Also seemingly gone are the days when top musicians like Oscar Pettiford let young musicians play with them and offered playing tips. Pianist

Bassist Anthony Cox is known throughout the jazz world but has chosen Minneapolis for his home.

Ken Green reminisced of a time when he and Rufus Webster were too young to get in the door at Near Northside clubs, but they "went in anyway and heard not only jam sessions with local musicians but experienced the camaraderie. Players from big bands would stop in . . . People would meet more, and all the musicians would be there. At Saturday afternoon jam sessions at Curly's on Fifth Street, they'd invite young guys to come up and sit in. That atmosphere doesn't exist anymore."

Venues for free jazz and avant-garde music still "shift with the wind," says Milo Fine, and established clubs like the Dakota and Artists' Quarter rarely present it. Galleries and bars shift booking policies to preclude the genre or go out of business. A few places such as the West Bank School of Music and Homewood Studios, an intimate gallery in North Minneapolis, offer opportunities to hear this music.

There are some notable exceptions. Today's Artists' Quarter regularly presents the Pete Whitman X-tet, a large contemporary ensemble, and young artists frequently get the opportunity to take the stage there. Bassist Anthony Cox, a Coon Rapids, Minnesota, native, paid his dues in New York but returned to the Twin Cities, playing with the Regional Trio or Quartet at the now defunct Turf Club's Clown Lounge, at the Artists' Quarter, and at other local nightspots.

The Turf Club's Monday night Jazz Implosion, once hosted by bassist Adam Linz, J. T. Bates, and Michael Lewis, for several years gained a reputation for a place to *hear* music, not carry on conversation. All of the five-dollar cover went to performers, and according to *City Pages*, "When somebody's playing, everybody listens—not just out of respect, but because that's what they're there for. No matter how quiet Fat Kid or their handpicked guest artists get, every note comes through, unsullied by chatter." The Clown Lounge closed its doors on New Year's Day, 2011.

Among the notable musicians playing in the Twin Cities is Prince Rogers Nelson—known as Prince when his pop career took off in the eighties and later simply as a "love symbol." Prince has continued to skirt the edges of jazz in the new century. His composition "West" from the 2003 *N.E.W.S.* album of instrumental music has been described as "a soothing jazz piece." His backup musicians have consistently been quality jazzers. Prince's roots in jazz date to his father, John Rogers, whose group was

The Bad Plus at the Dakota in downtown Minneapolis

known as the Prince Rogers Trio. Prince currently lives in Minneapolis (and is an avid Vikings and Timberwolves fan).

Drummer David King is the common denominator between the all-acoustic trio known as the Bad Plus and the "punk jazz" group Happy Apple. Both groups fuse jazz and other elements including rock and contemporary, though not free music. Bad Plus members also include pianist Ethan Iverson from Wisconsin and bassist Reid Anderson. Anderson and King are native Minneapolitans who also have musical outlets in New York. King has maintained a high profile in the Twin Cities. Both groups find considerable success with European audiences.

Happy Apple is made up of King, Michael Lewis on saxophone, and Erik Fratzke (originally from Winona, Minnesota) on electric bass. Lewis plays saxophone in the group known as Fat Kid Wednesdays at St. Paul's Turf Club. The *Minnesota Daily* reported that "Happy Apple pushes the

Happy Apple and Fat Kid Wednesdays saxophonist Michael Lewis

Adam Linz oversees the MacPhail Center for Music's jazz program and is a bassist on the contemporary Twin Cities scene.

envelope, albeit in a humble way, in an effort to turn jazz's art gallery syndrome on its ear."

Saxophonist Lewis, besides working with Happy Apple, fronts the edgy modern jazz trio Fat Kid Wednesdays with Adam Linz and drummer J. T. Bates. Richard Brody of the *New Yorker* called Lewis "one of the most intriguing and exhilarating young jazz musicians around." He has roots in the jazz of the 1960s with a definite Ornette Coleman influence, but he takes on a free jazz mantle unique to the new times. Happy Apple has performed with some frequency in France, where it has gained a following.

In 2009, bassist Adam Linz was named to head the jazz program at MacPhail Center for Music, now almost a century old. Like many Twin Cities musicians, Linz plays with myriad people and bands, including Fat Kid Wednesdays.

Veteran Twin Cities jazz man Dave Karr turned seventy as the new century dawned. He feels the local jazz scene is healthy and teeming with good writers and players: "I won't start naming names or I'll have trouble stopping. There are interesting, worth-paying-attention-to, world-class players on every instrument and, actually, plenty of jazz to hear. The avant garde is a small but really happening segment of jazz, but it's always been that way, hasn't it? Twin Cities' musicianship knocked me out when I first came here many years ago, and the place is still a hotbed of wonderful musicians."

Appendix

Goetting's Twin Cities All-Stars

The following is an admittedly subjective and non-scientific listing of the most significant jazz musicians to play the performance locations of Minneapolis and St. Paul over the years. It is based on responses to questionnaires sent out early in this project, mentions by colleagues, and references in the annals of the region's history. Birth and death years, when known, are included. Regardless of whether this compilation matches readers' preferences, these players helped enrich the jazz legacy of the Twin Cities. If they were to somehow be gathered together on a local stage, it would be one hell of a band.

SAX/FLUTE/REEDS

Tommy Bauer (1920–?)
Gary Berg (b. 1939)
Eddie Berger (1932–2008)
Harry Blons (1911–87)
Serge Chaloff (1923–57)
Bob Crea (1928–80)
Percy Hughes (b. 1922)
Ray Kammerer (d. 1939)
Dave Karr (b. 1930)
Jim Marentic (b. 1940?)
Frank Morgan (1933–2007)
Dick Pendleton (1918–99)

Margie Pettiford (1916–86)
Frankie Roberts (1905–98)
Bob Rockwell (b. 1945)
Irv Williams (b. 1919)
Lester Young (1909–59)

TRUMPET/CORNET

Bud Brisbois (1937–75)
Craig Buie (1901–?)
Jack Coan (b. 1930)
Paul "Doc" Evans (1907–77)
Rook Ganz (1904–79)
Jerry Rusch (1943–2003)

TROMBONE

Dave Graf
Stan Haugesag (1929–97)
Jerry Mullaney (d. 1980)
Bruce Paulson (b. 1944?)
Hal Runyon (1903–94)

PIANO

Bob Davis (1927–96)
Manfredo Fest (1936–99)
Dave Frishberg (b. 1933)
Bobby Lyle (b. 1944)
Mickey McClain (b. 1939)
Bobby Peterson (1950–2002)
Jeanne Arland Peterson (b. 1921?)
Butch Thompson (b. 1943)
Rufus Webster (1903–59?)
Sid Williams

DRUMS

George Avaloz (b. 1937)
Bill Blakkestad (1929–85?)
Jay Epstein (b. 1946)
Eric "Kamau" Gravatt (b. 1947)
Phil Hey
Kenny Horst (b. 1944?)
Russ Moore
Joe Pulice

GUITAR

Bob Caldwell
Mike Elliott (1940–2005)
Jerry Hubbard (b. 1934?)
Reuben Ristrom (b. 1943?)

BASS

Adolphus Alsbrook (1912–88)
Biddy Bastien (1908–2003)
Jim Hughart (b. 1936)
Gordy Johnson (b. 1952)
Billy Peterson (b. 1951)
Oscar Pettiford (1922–60)

VOCAL

Debbie Duncan
Shirley Forwood (b. 1935?)
Carole Martin
Dick Mayes
Patty McGovern
Patty Peterson (b. 1954)

ARRANGER

Boyd Atkins (c.1900–?)
Frank Lewis
Maria Schneider (b. 1960)
Tom Talbert (1924–2005)

Appendix

Music Venues over the Years

The Near Northside was a center of jazz and night life almost devoid of racial barriers from Prohibition until the intrusion of Highway 55. Construction of this road, later named the Floyd B. Olson Memorial Highway, resulted in the destruction of entire neighborhoods. Lester Young's family lived on Sixth Avenue North, and Frank Morgan's parents were nearby.

The **Apex** at 655 Sixth Avenue North dates back to at least 1933. It was doors away from the **Clef Club,** 637 Sixth Avenue North in the Kistler Building, where the **Halfway Club** was up a flight of stairs and the **Ebony Social Club** was on the third floor. **Club DeLiza** was across the street. Not far down Highland was the **Black Elks** club and **Ames Lodge,** also known as the **Musicians Rest.** It became the **Harlem Breakfast Club,** a black and tan after-hours rib place, at 141 Highland Avenue in 1934. The **Boulevard** and the **Hub** were farther west on Sixth Avenue North near Dupont.

Howard's Steak House at 715 Sixth Avenue North was the stuff of legends, a hub of activity until the mid-fifties. It was also known as **El Grotto** and **Howard's Club Jazz Bar** (in the early fifties), but its reputation was set in the 1930s, when Lester Young, the Pettifords, and traveling bands like Ellington and Eli Rice would hang out there after hours. Ma and Pa Pettiford ran the **Old Southern Barbecue** at 700 North Lyndale. The nearby **Just Right Barbeque** was said to have better ribs but no music.

Many places around the country were called the **Cotton Club.** Minneapolis had at least two. The **Cotton Club Chicken Shack** at 718 Sixth

Avenue North, on the north side of Olson Highway between Lyndale Avenue and Lyndale Place, was the site of an infamous cop killing in 1928. It became known as **Club Kongo** in 1933 and just a year later was renamed **Club Morocco.** Other night spots within walking distance were Ben Wilson's **Gin Mill** (1940s) on North Lyndale, the **Kitty Cat Klub** on Sixth Avenue North between Highland and Aldrich, the **Nest** at 731 Sixth Avenue North, **Peggy's** after-hours club, **Rhumboogie** (1945–46; previously the **Maple Leaf**) at 128 Highland, and the **Wondervue** on Sixth Avenue North. The best known of the Twin Cities' **Cotton Clubs,** of course, was also called **El Patio,** located at 5916 Excelsior Boulevard in St. Louis Park, where Lester Young, Rook Ganz, Boyd Atkins, and others played in the 1930s.

Hennepin Avenue in Minneapolis ran the gamut from seedy dives to posh theaters, but it has always been a center for musical activity. Considered a gem among U.S. vaudeville houses, the **Hennepin Orpheum** opened at 910 Hennepin in 1921. The **State Theatre,** described as a "gilded pleasure palace," was built the same year at 805 Hennepin. The **Minnesota Theater** at Eighth and LaSalle boasted its own orchestra. On the current site of **Orchestra Hall** on Eleventh Street sat the **Lyceum,** once home to road shows. Dating to 1905, it was the first building in the complex that would become the **Minneapolis Auditorium.** Most of the vaudeville theaters later did burlesque, notably the **Alvin** near Fifth and Hennepin. The **Palace Theater** at 414 Hennepin presented many of the big bands of the Swing Era.

Musicians would hit the Avenue after their performances and find opportunities to sit in at the **Camel's Club,** 520 Hennepin, or the **Paradise** right next door, or **Lindy's** (aka **Crombie's**). Also nearby was the **Dome,** which became **Vic's** and later **Osterberg's,** at 507 Hennepin. **Lindy's** gave way to **Augie's,** one of the first strip clubs, which was followed by the **Copper Squirrel,** the **Gay '90s,** the **Frolics,** the **Saddle,** and the **Roaring Twenties,** each of which employed jazz groups.

It wasn't all scantily clad women, however. Herman Mitch's **Casablanca** at 408 Hennepin had some of the best Dixie in town, as did the nearby **Red Feather** at Fourth and Hennepin and **Williams** at Ninth and Hennepin. **Robert's Cafe** on East Hennepin also featured live music. In earlier years, a pair of labor temples on the east side of the Mississippi featured bands. Other establishments with music included the **Poodle, Sleizer's, Spud's,** and the **Coconut Grove** over **Brady's,** where you could "Walk up a flight and save a dollar." In 1930, the **Gallery** at Eighth and Hennepin featured Art Goldberg, who came to be known as Hollywood writer Arthur Morton, on piano.

Later, the hot spots included the **Bellanote** at Sixth and Hennepin and **Taffy's,** with its name entertainment just off the Avenue on Sixth. If you ventured as far as Lake Street, **Le Zoo** offered a coffeehouse setting for young jazz artists in the sixties. **Williams Pub** was also nearby in the Uptown area. Farther west on Hennepin is the Walker Art Center complex, which once housed the **Tyrone Guthrie Theater,** which hosted such jazz artists as Bill Evans, Miles Davis, and Charles Mingus.

Minneapolis hotels with music included the **Radisson, Leamington, Curtis, Nicollet, Normandy,** and **Hastings,** known for its **Mar-Key Club.**

The area around the University of Minnesota was a haven for jazz sounds over the years. The fraternity and sorority houses were often party central, and, once the **Boogie Woogie Club** broke ground in the early 1940s, campus locations opened up to modern music, including **Coffman Student Union** itself. In Dinkytown, **Valli Pizza** presented small groups; Steve Kimmell's **Rainbow Gallery** on the West Bank housed modern and experimental sounds; and the **Big Ten, Cafe Extempore,** and **Tempo** also featured live music.

To keep things interesting, St. Paul and Minneapolis boasted several establishments with common names but different owners and clienteles. Both cities had a **Wagon Wheel,** complete with music offerings. Both had the **Flame:** St. Paul's at Eighth and Wabasha, where Charlie Parker and other jazz greats played in the 1950s; Minneapolis's at 1523 Nicollet. Duluth also had the **Flame Supper Club,** on London Road, a classy joint to which Twin Cities musicians would often travel three hours for gigs. None of these should be confused with the **Radisson Hotel's Flame Room.**

St. Paul had its theater scene, too. Built in 1910 at 10 East Exchange Street, the **Fitzgerald,** originally called the **Sam S. Shubert Theater,** is the city's oldest surviving theater space. The **New Palace Theater** opened in 1916 at 19–21 West Seventh Street. It changed its name to the **Palace Orpheum** in 1922, then became the **Orpheum,** and then the **RKO Orpheum.** Across the street was the **Paramount.** Sally Ordway put up the first $7.5 million for construction of the facility at 345 Washington Street that bears her name; the **Ordway Center for the Performing Arts** opened in 1985.

The **Artists' Quarter** began at Twenty-sixth and Lake Street in Minneapolis, moved to the basement of the McColl Building in downtown St. Paul in 1995, and more recently relocated to the nearby Hamm Building. The **Dakota** started life in St. Paul's Bandana Square but now calls Minneapolis's Nicollet Mall home.

St. Paul's hotels have long been band headquarters, from the early broadcasts at the St. Paul Hotel's **Gopher Grill** and **Spanish Room** and the Lowry's **Terrace Café** to the **Commodore,** where the Wolverines held sway. Other downtown locations include the **French Press,** the **Lower Levee Lounge, Castle Royal** in the mushroom caves, and **Miller's Club,** where Wally Olson's band played for more than a decade and which later became the **Colony Club** and **Matt Weber's.**

University Avenue was home to the **Coliseum Ballroom** at Lexington, where Ellington and other great bands performed. The **Prom Ballroom** stood close by from 1941 until its demise in 1987. **Heinie's,** later **Alary's,** was at University and Virginia, near the **Boulevards of Paris.** The **Silver Stripe** resided at Dale. To the north was **Allen's Tavern** near **Swing City,** where Kid Cann had ties and Rook Ganz performed, at 1682 Rice Street and the **Depot** near Lake Johanna. Lester Young once played at **Happy Hollow** on Rice Street. The **Minnesota Music Café** has been at 449 Payne Avenue since 1997. The **Golden Steer** in South St. Paul featured Cornbread Harris.

The suburbs and the outlands welcomed jazz and big bands at places like the **Hotel Del Otero** at Spring Lake Park, Lake Minnetonka, **Big Reggie's,** the **Down Beat,** the **Lakeview,** and the **Spring Park Casino.** There was **Adolph's** in Robbinsdale; St. Louis Park's **Ambassador; Bar Harbor, Breezy Point,** the **Quarter Deck,** and the **Country Club** on Bay Lake near Brainerd; and the **Bull Pen** and **Main Street** in Hopkins. Journalist and broadcaster Cedric Adams featured music occasionally, and he even sat in on drums at **Cedric's** restaurant in Edina. Fargo's **Crystal Ballroom** hosted the big bands of the thirties, forties, and fifties. Others were the **Hopkins House,** the **White House** (once the original **Turf Club** with its **Clown Lounge**), and the **Point** in Golden Valley; **Medina Ballroom, Park Terrace,** and the **Plantation** in White Bear; and the **"Y"** in Chaska. Duluth venues included **Green's Crystal Terrace** and the **Lennox Hotel.**

The tiny hamlet of Mendota housed the **Bow and Arrow**, the **Colonial**, the **Emporium of Jazz, Gay Paree, Mitch's**, Red Dougherty's **Parker House**, the **Ragin' Cajun, Rampart Street Club**, and the **River Road Club.**

Others in and around downtown Minneapolis included **Big Al's, Blue Note, Blue Ox, Cafe Extraordinaire, Cafe Luxx, Cassius Bar, Club Carnival, Curly's, Davey Jones' Locker, Diamond Lil's, Duff's, Duffy's Fine Line, Fox and Hounds, Freddie's**, the **Gaslight, Golden Pheasant, Golliwog Lounge, Happy Hour, Herb's, Hoop-D-Doo, Jazzmines, Jockey Club, Key Club (South of the Border), King Solomon's Mines**, the **Longhorn, Loon, Magoo's, Marigold Ballroom, Music Box, Nankin, Nicky's, Persian Palms, Pierre's**, the **President Café, Ramona, Rossi's Blue Star Room, Roxy, Rusty Nail**, the **Spot, Sweet Georgia Brown's, Swinging Door, Times, 26 Club, Variety Bar.**

Additional St. Paul venues: **Acme Palm Garden, B&R, Belmont, Chang O'Hara's, Coleman's, Ebony Lounge, Green's Place, Mancini's**, the **Manor, Mauer's, Oxford Ballroom, Paramount Inn, Roadbuddy's, Than's, Treasure Inn, Venetian Inn**, and the **Zephyr.**

Of course, there are dozens more, and a few of them deserve at least honorable mention: **Anglessy, Arcadia Gardens, Arthur's, Big Daddy's**, the **Bronco Bar, Bucky's, Calhoun Beach Hotel, Club 350, Como Park Pavilion, Criterion, Dew Drop Inn, Diamond Jim's, Drum Bar, Goofy's, Hafners, Hanson House, Hap's**, the **Hub, Iron Horse, Lake Harriet Band Shell, Lee and Eddie's, Loon, Manor, McGuire's, Mr. C's, 'Nando's Hideaway**, the **Owl, Padded Cell, Someplace Else, Trocadero**, and the **Whole.**

Notes on Sources

Much of the material in this book is drawn from interviews conducted by Dave Sletten and Kent Hazen and aired on KBEM. For interviews not gathered by the Sletten-Hazen team, additional details are noted.

Leigh Kamman was a regular contact for background information and fact-checking for this project. His *Jazz in the Cities,* a two-part program on Minnesota Public Radio, also supplied a good deal of information. Kent Hazen generously shared his knowledge and connections throughout the course of researching and writing this book.

Sources are listed by chapter, below. The interviews that informed each chapter are listed first, followed by print and online sources, keyed to the text where necessary for clarity. Many manuscript sources are held in the collection slated for donation to the Minnesota Historical Society.

Cruising Up the River

Interviews: Tela Burt, February 1993; Rufus Webster, c. 1994 (on St. Paul Hotel); Roy Robison, by Carl Warmington, September 5, 1987; Dave Faison, c. 1994; Ken Green, March 1994.

For details on riverboat music, particularly Fate Marable, Louis Armstrong, Boyd Atkins, and Bix Beiderbecke (p. 126), see William Howland Kenney, *Jazz on the River* (Chicago: University of Chicago Press, 2005). On Jelly Roll Morton, see Benny Goodman and Irving Kolodin, *The Kingdom of Swing* (Mechanicsburg, PA: Stackpole, 1939). The "old-timer" (p. 6) was John Kalbrener, interviewed in August 2007. Armstrong calls the riverboats his "university," from Dennis Owsley, *City of Gabriels: The History of Jazz in St. Louis, 1895–1973* (St. Louis, MO: Reedy Press, 2006). On the Original Dixieland Jass Band, see Geoffrey C. Ward and Ken Burns, *Jazz: A History of America's Music* (New York: Knopf, 2000), and Marshall W. Stearns, *The Story of Jazz* (New York: Oxford University Press, 1956).

For more on riverboats, see Letha C. Greene, *Long Live the Delta Queen* (New York: Hastings House Publishers, 1973). During World War II, the *Delta Queen* was in the service of the U.S. Navy until August 1945, when it was declared surplus and sold to the Greene Line, based in Cincinnati. It was returned to New Orleans and plied the waters of the Mississippi once again, veering off the main channel to take the St. Croix River up to Stillwater, all the while with live music on board.

Jazz, Jazz Everywhere

Interviews: Frankie Roberts, February 1994; Tela Burt, February 1993; Jeanne Arland Peterson, c. 1994; Eddie Tolck, c. 1994; Butch Thompson, John Kujawa and Russ Roth, 1994; Roy Robison, by Carl Warmington, September 5, 1987; Robison, September 1994; Carl Warmington, August 1993; Warmington, by author, September 19, 1987; Arthur Morton (by phone from Hollywood), c. 1994; Craig Buie, by Carl Warmington, December 8, 1987; Les Beigel, by Carl Warmington, September 19, 1987; Hal Runyon, by Carl Warmington, September 4, 1987.

Volstead details from Eric Dregni, Mark Moran, and Mark Sceurman, *Weird Minnesota* (New York: Sterling Publishing Co., 2006). A flavor of the era comes from Riverwalk Jazz, "Jazz Notes—Speakeasies, Flappers & Red Hot Jazz: Music of the Prohibition" (n.d.), http://www.riverwalkjazz.org/. Further details about gangsters in the Twin Cities can be found in Paul Maccabee, *John Dillinger Slept Here: A Crooks' Tour of Crime and Corruption in St. Paul, 1920–1936* (St. Paul: Minnesota Historical Society Press, 1995). Nettie Hayes Sherman stories from Lori Rotenberk, "Nettie Hayes Sherman Can Still Play Just About Anything," *Twin Cities Magazine*, February 1982. Kidd Cann as "overlord" from St. Louis Park Historical Society, http://www.slphistory.org/history/kidcann.asp. Davie Berman details from Susan Berman, *Easy Street* (New York: Dial Press, 1981).

Marigold Gardens history available in the documentary *Lost Twin Cities* (St. Paul, MN: Twin Cities Public Television, 1995). Como Theater details from *Minneapolis Journal* series on Paul Whiteman, August 15, 1926. *Min-*

nesota Daily ads from archive, c. 1918. Article by Russell Roth published in *Minneapolis Tribune,* (n.d.) 1952. On the Radisson, see *A History of the Radisson Hotel, Downtown Minneapolis* (Minneapolis, MN: Carlson Companies, 1998). Buie on the Randall band is from Dick Raichelson's liner notes, *Twin Cities Shuffle* (Arcadia, catalog no. 2016). Les Beigel story in part from Carl Warmington, "Jazz Memories," essay. Beigel article, *DownBeat Magazine,* 1937.

The Near Northside

Interviews: Arthur Morton, c. 1994; W. Harry Davis, c. 1994; Pete Karalis, on *Jazz in the Cities,* Minnesota Public Radio, 1978; Frankie Roberts, February 1994; Ted Unseth, on *Jazz in the Cities,* Minnesota Public Radio, 1978; Tommy Bauer, 1993; Dave Faison, c. 1993 and 1994 (including Ganz story); Butch Thompson, John Kujawa, and Russ Roth, 1994 (Maddock quote); Jerry Mullaney, on *Jazz in the Cities,* Minnesota Public Radio, 1978.

Residents living "outside the law" from *Minneapolis Journal,* October 28, 1925. El Patio details supplied by Kent Hazen and St. Louis Park Historical Society website, http://www.slphistory.org/history/eb5916.asp. *National Geographic* quote from March 1935 issue. Ted Unseth's comments from his website, http://tedeboy.tripod.com/acjo/. C. K. Running letter, Minnesota Historical Society archives, St. Paul.

Prejudice in a Progressive Setting

Interviews: Tela Burt, February 1993; James Samuel Harris II, c. 1994; W. Harry Davis, c. 1994; Ken Green, March 23, 1994; Roy Robison, September 1994, and by Carl Warmington, September 5, 1987; Dave Faison, c. 1993 and 1994; Irv Williams, with author, videotaped by Lee Sandberg, February 14, 2008; Dick Mayes, with author, July 2008; Bill Schneider and Eddie Tolck, c. 1994.

Statistics on African American population and details about economic opportunities in the Twin Cities from David Vassar Taylor, "The Blacks," in *They Chose Minnesota: A Survey of the State's Ethnic Groups,* ed. June D. Holmquist (St. Paul: Minnesota Historical Society Press, 1976). Musical history credited to Judy M. Henderson from *African-American Music in Minnesota: From Spirituals to Rap,* CD (St. Paul: Minnesota Historical Society Press, 1994). Also see Rotenberk, "Nettie Hayes Sherman." Details on local segregation history from Lori Sturdevant, ed., *Overcoming: The*

Autobiography of W. Harry Davis (Afton, MN: Afton Historical Society Press, 2002).

The Eli Rice band known as the Cotton Pickers is not to be confused with drummer William McKinney's group of the same name. The latter was much better known, having gained a national reputation through recordings on the Bluebird and Victor labels in the twenties. Based in Wisconsin and Michigan much of the time, the Rice band was booked by the Stecker Brothers Agency in the early 1930s and made several appearances in the Twin Cities with Ira Pettiford in the trumpet section.

The Musicians' Unions

Interviews: Carl Warmington, August 1993; Roy Robison, September 1994, and by Carl Warmington, September 5, 1987; Dave Faison, c. 1993 and 1994; Kenny Horst, with author, April 15, 2010; Leigh Kamman, with author, 2009; James A. Robb, Jr., by Carl Warmington, August 7, 1991; Hal Runyon, by Carl Warmington, September 4, 1987; Adolphus Alsbrook, by Lewis Porter, c. 1995; Ken Green, March 1994; Jack McDuff, 1994.

Julie Ayer, *More Than Meets the Ear: How Symphony Musicians Made Labor History* (Minneapolis, MN: Syren Book Co., 2005). Don Lang, *DownBeat Magazine*, January 1942. Details on the musicians' strike's end from *The Billboard*, February 24, 1945. Biddy Bastien's work for the union is drawn from David Bastien, "Biography of Ovid 'Biddy' Bastien," manuscript, c. 2005. Dick Kadrie's presidency listed in *Twin Cities Musicians Union Newsletter*, July 11, 2003. Joe Kimball story from "The Mature Musician—Music for Life: A Column Devoted to the Life Members of Local 30–73," AFM. Doc Evans quote from Mark Flaherty, "The Life and Music of Paul Wesley 'Doc' Evans (1907–1977)," *International Trumpet Guild Journal* (October, 2003). Jerry Swanberg quote from Twin Cities Jazz Society newsletter, n.d. Tom Baskerville quote from e-mailed correspondence with the author. Brad Eggen on the American Federation of Musicians is taken from an e-mailed response to author, May 14, 2010. More on Twin Cities Youth Jazz Camp can be found at the group's website, http://www.tcyjazzcamp.com/.

On the Avenue

Interviews: Tela Burt, February 1993; Percy Hughes, c. 1994; Russ Moore, c. 1994; Eddie Berger, 1994 (including details about Augie Ratner); Reuben Ristrom, with author, 2009 (for story linking Lee Pierson and Father Bill McGrade); Jan Jacobson, c. 1994; Gary Berg, c. 1994; Ron Seaman, with author, 2008; Dave Karr, with author, July 30, 2010; George Avaloz, 1994; Jeanne Pettiford, May 1994 (on Louis Bellson's family).

Paul Whiteman interview reported in *Minneapolis Sunday Tribune,* (n.d.) 1928. For Doc Evans on the 1928 Whiteman concert, see Paige Van-Vorst, "Doc Evans' Centennial: 1907–2007," http://www.docevans.com/Centennial.htm. Les Saefke on Whiteman is from "When Swing was King at the Orpheum," *Hennepin History* 50.4 (Fall 1991). Jim Trost recollections from "An Excerpt from the Memoirs of Jim Trost," available at Arkansas Jazz Heritage Foundation website, http://www.arjazz.org/archive/articles/jtrost/j_trost.html. Trost eventually moved to New Mexico, then to Little Rock, Arkansas, where he died of cancer in 1994.

For the Orpheum Theatre's history, see Saefke, "When Swing was King," and Hennepin Theatre Trust, www.hennepintheatretrust.org/. For more on the Minneapolis Urban League, see its website: www.mul.org/. On the "Many well-known Twin Cities musicians" and "keeping live music," see Bastien, "Biography of Ovid 'Biddy' Bastien." For more on the "jazz war," see *DownBeat Magazine,* 1954. Brad Eggen commented on the AFM litigation by e-mail, September 9, 2009.

Much of the Berger history came from the interview cited above as well as from other musicians' communications. Jack Landin story taken from completed questionnaire developed by author. Stan Scott reminiscence from a collection of vignettes gathered by Kent Hazen. Marian Haugesag's written recollections. On the Red Feather integration, see *DownBeat Magazine,* November 1941 and January 1944.

Twin Cities Jazz Celebs

Interviews: Leonard Phillips, by Bryant Dupre, transcribed and edited by Lewis Porter, January 1983; Pete Karalis, on *Jazz in the Cities,* Minnesota Public Radio, 1978; Dick Pendleton, c. 1994; Dirk Fischer, c. 1994; Adolphus Alsbrook, by Lewis Porter, 1986; Ken Green, March 1994; Tommy Bauer, September 10, 1993; Arthur Morton, Frankie Roberts, and Roy Robison, c. 1994 (on the Cotton Pickers); Dick Norling on *Jazz in the Cities,* Minnesota Public Radio, 1978; Leigh Kamman, with author, 2009; Bill Fitch, memoir/interview, c. 1965; Dave Faison, c. 1993 and 1994.

On Lester Young, see Douglas Henry Daniels, *Lester Leaps In: The Life and Times of Lester "Pres" Young* (Boston, MA: Beacon Press, 2002), and Lewis Porter, ed., *A Lester Young Reader* (Washington, DC: Smithsonian Institution, 1991). Leonard Phillips and Phil Phillips quotes from Frank Büchmann-Møller, *You Just Fight for Your Life: The Story of Lester Young* (New York: Praeger Publishers, 1990). On Twin Cities locations, see Lewis Porter, *Lester Young* (Ann Arbor: University of Michigan Press, 2005). Percy Hughes quote from *Song of the Spirit,* film, written and produced by Bruce Fredericksen (1988). Besides the citations noted, much of the material on Lester Young, including the Count Basie story, was found in the files of the Institute of Jazz Studies, Rutgers University, Newark, New Jersey.

On Adolphus Alsbrook, including details from his son Darryl and from Gerald Wiggins, see Duke Ellington Music Society bulletin: http://www.depanorama.net/dems/. Paul de Barros, *Jackson Street After Hours: The Roots of Jazz in Seattle* (Seattle, WA: Sasquatch Press; 1993). Charles Mingus and Nel King, *Beneath the Underdog: His World as Composed by Mingus* (New York: Random House, 1971). For "You don't mess with him" comment by Gerald Wiggins, see Duke Ellington Music Society website, cited above. Ray Fitch's recollections shared by his son, Ray, in a manuscript dating to c. 1970.

On Oscar Pettiford, listen to *Piano Jazz,* hosted by Marian McPartland, National Public Radio, January 29, 2010. George Hoefer, "Oscar Pettiford," *DownBeat Magazine,* June 2, 1966. Dizzy Gillespie quote from Ira Gitler, *The Masters of Bebop: A Listener's Guide* (Cambridge, MA: Da Capo Press, 2001). On the musical siblings, see C. Albertson, "Review of Sherrie Tucker's 'Swing Shift,'" *The New Crisis,* November 2000, and on Leontine in particular, see Eric Wendell, *Encyclopedia of Jazz Musicians,* at http://www.jazz.com/encyclopedia. Bastien, "Biography of Ovid 'Biddy' Bastien." "Oscar Pettiford was attracting broad attention" details from Hans-Joachim Schmidt, themen Verlag Köln, "Oscar Pettiford, 1922–1945," http://themenschmidt.de/oscar45.htm. Pettiford's first recording: Whitney Balliett, *Collected Works: A Journal of Jazz, 1954–2000* (New York: St. Martin's Press, 2000). Jerry Newhouse statement from Gitler, *Masters of Bebop.* On Jimmy Blanton, see "George Hoefer's Hot Box," *DownBeat Magazine,* June 1960. Milt Hinton quotes from Bill Crow, *Jazz Anecdotes* (New York: Oxford University Press, 1990), and career path from Scott DeVeaux, *The*

Birth of Bebop: A Social and Musical History (Berkeley: University of California Press, 1997). Frank Büchmann-Møller, *Someone to Watch Over Me: The Life and Music of Ben Webster* (Ann Arbor: University of Michigan Press, 2006). Besides the citations noted, much of the material on Oscar Pettiford was found in the files of the Institute of Jazz Studies, Rutgers University, Newark, New Jersey.

On Frank Morgan, see Andrea Canter, "Frank Morgan, 1933–2007," Jazz Police, http://www.jazzpolice.com/content/view/7452/79/.

On Serge Chaloff, see Bob McCaffery, "With Serge Chaloff in Minneapolis," manuscript, May 2000, held at his home in Little Falls, NJ, and Patrick Fitzgerald, "Playing Jazz in the Twin Cities, 1943–1951," manuscript.

Way Up North in Dixieland

Interviews: Meredith "Mickey" McClain, with author, 2008; Allen Evans, with author, November 17, 2007 (on Paul "Doc" Evans biography); Leigh Kamman, with author, 2009; Eddie Tolck, c. 1994; Eric Giere, Jeanne Peterson, Bill Schneider (remembering Harry Blons), c. 1994; Dick Pendleton, c. 1994; Butch Thompson, c. 1994; Bill Schneider, c. 1994 (including Bob Greunenfelder quote); Jimmy Robb and Frankie Roberts, c. 1994 (details about Norvy Mulligan and Dick Pendleton); Charlie DeVore and others, n.d. (including history of Hall Brothers band).

Bastien Dixieland recollection from "Biography of Ovid 'Biddy' Bastien." On venues where Doc Evans played, see Flaherty, "Life and Music of Paul Wesley 'Doc' Evans." On Evans at Mitch's, see Paul "Doc" Evans, "Jazz and Swing in the Thirties," *Mississippi Rag*, January 1979. Doc Evans on trends reported by Russell Roth in *Minneapolis Tribune* (n.d.). Butch Thompson quote on Evans comes from the liner notes for the album *Four or Five Times*.

Caption quote from Jerry Mullaney (p. 110): *Jazz in the Cities*, Minnesota Public Radio, 1978. Ervin "Red" Wolfe biography courtesy Rueben Ristrom, e-mailed correspondence, July 8, 2010.

From Swing to Bebop and Beyond

Interviews: Irv Williams, with author, videotaped by Lee Sandberg, February 14, 2008; David Karr, 1993, and with author, July 30, 2010; Herb Pilhofer, Hal Lichterman, Russ Moore, and Dave Karr, c. 1994.

Rufus Webster on Irv Williams and Williams on traveling gigs collected by Tom Surowicz for *Jazz Masters Journal* (1995). The Bastien family biography comes from *Jazz in the Cities*, Minnesota Public Radio, 1978.

The Clubs

Interviews: Dick Driscoll and others, c. 1994 (on Mitch's); Kenny Horst, with author, April 15, 2010; Jim Marentic, with author, 2008; Dave Frishberg, c. 1995; Dave Karr, 1993, and with author, July 30, 2010 (including details about Trevor Koehler and Les Rout); Russ Peterson and Ron Seaman, c. 1994; Meredith "Mickey" McClain, with author, 2008; Maurice Turner and Jack Kryzinski, c. 1994; Reuben Ristrom, with author, 2009.

On Harry Blons's band, see Bill Schneider, *The Mississippi Rag*, July 1982. On the fire and Paul Warburton's bass, see Bass Forum online, http://www.smithbassforums.com/showthread.php?t=339. For Robert Rockwell quotes, see Bob Protzman, "Profile of Robert Rockwell," *Down-Beat Magazine*, November 4, 1976. Peterson family history gleaned from Jeanne Arland Peterson eightieth birthday video, available at http://www.youtube.com/watch?v=5b8n9pfDxKs. Billy Holloman website: http://www.billyholloman.com/. Perry Peoples's comments from completed questionnaire developed by author. Kent Hazen's recollections on Thelonious Monk are from e-mailed correspondence, 2010. For Dakota club history, see Britt Robson, "Planet Pickett," *The Rake*, February 2008, and Chris Roberts, *State of the Arts: Jazz*, Minnesota Public Radio, October 30, 2002. On acts at the Guthrie Theater, see Stan Haugesag, *Reflections on the Last 50 Years of TC Jazz*, c. 1990. Gary Berg quoted in *Brew: The Hamm's Magazine for Tavern Owners*, May-June 1961. George Avaloz biographical details from liner notes by Tom Surowicz, *The Highest Mountain*, 2004.

The Big Bands

Interviews: Bill Schneider, c. 1994; Stan Haugesag, Dick Whitbeck, Brett Forberg, Frank Bencriscutto, Steve Wright, and John Zdechlik, c. 1994; Tom Morgan, from *Jazz in the Cities*, Minnesota Public Radio, c. 1975; Maurice Turner and Jack Kryzinski, c. 1994; Percy Hughes, 1995, and with author, 2008; Maria Schneider, c. 1995, 1996; Irv Williams, with author, videotaped by Lee Sandberg, February 14, 2008.

On Bud Brisbois, see Kevin Seeley's entry at http://www.seeleymusic

.com/brisbois/brisart.htm. The history of the Dybvig band was told by Will Jones, "Death of a Band," *Minneapolis Sunday Tribune*, August 12, 1956. John Zdechlik shares details of "The Denny Murphy Band" in a piece written for the author, 2009. Details on the "Parade of Jazz" provided by Arnie Ness and Norm Staska via e-mail, July 2010. Details on the Glad Olinger Band are from Tom (Tippy) Morgan, Camarillo, CA, October 1998. For more on the Wolverines, see Dave Sletten, "The Wolverines Classic Jazz Orchestra," at http://tedeboy.tripod.com/id40.html. On Percy Hughes as a mail carrier, see United States Tennis Association Northern, online newsletter, reprinted by Minneapolis Central High School, also available on "Out and About in Richfield," produced for public access television, 2008; Tom Talbert's biography was written by Bruce Talbot: *Tom Talbert, His Life and Times: Voices from a Vanished World of Jazz* (Lanham, MD: Scarecrow Press, 2004).

The Singers

Interviews: Dick Pendleton, c. 1994 (on vocalists Barbara Hughes, Jane Green, and Kelly Stoneman); Leigh Kamman, with author, 2009.

George Avaloz quoted by Bill Gardner, *St. Paul Pioneer Press*, June 15, 2003. Details on Peggy Lee's life from Chuck Haga, *Minneapolis Star Tribune*, January 24, 2002. *Billboard Magazine*, November 3, 1956. On Bonnie Herman, see Twin Cities Musician Union, "This Month's Musician," *Duet*, 2002. Jim Trost recollections from "An Excerpt from the Memoirs." Jon Bream quote from Andrea Canter, "Carole Martin Warms the Artists' Quarter," www.jazzpolice.com/content/view/8649/115/. Will Jones column, "After Last Night," *Minneapolis Tribune*, c. 1960s. Phil Hey quoted in Chris Roberts, *State of the Arts: Jazz*, Minnesota Public Radio, October 30, 2002.

Jazz on the Air

Interviews: Hal Runyon, by Carl Warmington, September 4, 1987 (also reporting on Frankie Roberts and Vince Bastien); Leigh Kamman, with author, 2009; Percy Hughes, c. 1994; Eddie Berger, 1994.

Walter Winchell quote from "George Putnam, 1914–2008," on New Nixon blog, http://blog.nixonfoundation.org/2008/09/george-putnam-1914-2008/. "An Open Letter to St. Paul from Garrison Keillor," *St. Paul*

Pioneer Press, July 6, 1999. Henry Busse details from *Connect Business Magazine,* http://connectbiz.com/2001/11/shuffle-rhythmcom-henry-busse-jr/. *Mississippi Rag* available at http://www.mississippirag.com/aboutrag.html.

Jazz in the New Millennium

Interviews: Milo Fine, by e-mail with author, July 26, 2010; Ken Green, n.d.

On jazz education, see Stan Haugesag, *Reflections on the Last 50 Years.* "Listeners have to make an effort" from *Jazz in the Cities,* Minnesota Public Radio, c. 1970s. Turf Club details from *City Pages,* Best of the Twin Cities 2010. *Minnesota Daily* quoted in Phil DiPietro, "What Part of the Solution Problem Don't You Understand? Happy Apple Bassman Erik Fratzke Refrains From Fronting," http://www.allaboutjazz.com/iviews/efratzke2002.htm. Richard Brody, "Jazz Week: Fat Kid Wednesdays (French Connection 1)," *The New Yorker,* May 13, 2008. On Adam Linz, see Pamela Espeland, "MacPhail Names Adam Linz to Lead Jazz Program," *MinnPost,* June 8, 2009. Dave Karr shared his thoughts via e-mail, July 31, 2010.

Index

Page numbers in *italic* refer to captions and illustrations

Illustration Credits

Pages 4, 5, 165	Minnesota Historical Society collections
Page 7	Courtesy Duncan Schiedt
Page 10	Courtesy H. Schreiber
Pages 54, 68, 74, 119, 134, 135, 137, 143, 174, 176, 181, 189, 193, 195, 196, 197	Courtesy Andrea Canter
Page 116	Courtesy Dick Parker
Page 167	*Star Tribune,* Minnesota Historical Society collections

All other images from Dave Sletten–Kent Hazen collection

Printed in the USA
CPSIA information can be obtained
at www.ICGtesting.com
JSHW082159140824
68134JS00014B/321